I0437027

What Ever Happened to Sally

By

Dekota R. Cagle

This book is a work of fiction. Places, events, and situations in this story are purely fictional. Any resemblance to actual persons, living or dead, is coincidental.

© 2005 by Dekota R. Cagle. All rights reserved.

No part of this book may be reproduced, stored in a retrireview system, or transmitted by any means, electronic, mechanical, photocopying, recording, or otherwise, without written permission from the author.

First published by AuthorHouse 01/26/05

ISBN: 1-4208-9970-8 (e-book)
ISBN: 1-4208-9969-4 (soft)

This book is printed on acid free paper.

CHAPTER 1

When the phone rang, I answered by saying, "State Game Warden." The man on the other end of the line was a local land owner whom I had helped with hunting problems before.

"Yes," I said. "Yes, I am quite familiar with where you are talking about. And on which side of the creek did you hear the dogs?" I asked… "Yes sir," I said, "I'll be there as soon as I possibly can."

Rushing through the house, I grabbed for my shirt and pistol belt at the same time. Still trying to push on my right boot, I stepped out onto the wooden porch. I stood erect after adjusting my boot and began snapping my belt keepers down on my leather gun belt.

I took a deep breath. The air was still filled with the moisture from the spring thunderstorm that had just passed. Lightning slashes still darted across the sky in the east as the storm moved on. The smell of spring was strong after the rain. It seemed more true to me than ever that "April showers bring May flowers."

I jogged across the yard to my Game Warden truck. Jumping in, I fastened my seat belt, and at the same time, started the engine. I had received these kinds of calls before during my sixteen years as a Game Warden, but as I had gotten older, this kind of call became more important to me.

Spinning the truck around in the yard, I turned the headlights on and started out of the driveway. The steam was rising from the black asphalt road as I reached the end of the driveway. The low, foggy conditions would delay my arrival time and could possibly interfere with actually making direct contact with the people I was so desperate to catch. I was driving as fast as I thought was safe, yet everything along the old clay road seemed to be passing in slow motion. I recited the "better late than never" proverb to myself. I had driven to within a mile of my destination and started down the long sloping hill headed to the creek bottom below. Thinking I would save more time if I took a short-cut, I had taken a road that I normally would not have taken.

The steep, sloping banks along the old country road were now higher than the top of my truck. I came down this particular road hoping to intercept another vehicle coming out of the creek bottom. The chances of meeting any vehicle at 1:00 a.m. would be slim. Plus, being twenty miles from town made those chances even less. If I met any vehicle at all, it would probably be the people I was looking for.

Noticing no other tracks on the road, my hopes were still very high that I would intercept a vehicle— any vehicle. I would now have probable cause to stop any vehicle I met simply by the information I received on the phone.

I managed to make it to the bottom of the muddy hill and started to go across an old angling wooden bridge. As I crossed the bridge, the damp wood seemed unusually slick as my truck started to slide sideways. I didn't know if I was sliding because the bridge timbers were wet or from all the mud that had managed to build up around my tires. The thought did flash through my mind though, that maybe it was my speed that caused me to lose control on the wet wood and slide. I released the gas pedal under my foot and shuffle-steered back into the center of the road at the opposite end of the bridge. To my left I noticed a hole about fifteen feet deep where the roadside had caved off near the end of the bridge I had just crossed. After taking a quick, deep breath, I said to myself, "I'm glad the bridge wasn't longer." After this, my mind quickly went back to the business at hand. I knew this area well and decided I would arrive where I was needed in less than two minutes.

The end of Mr. Crowe's driveway had just become visible, easily recognized by an old metal pole with a wagon wheel that had been placed flat and attached to the top of the pole. On top of the wheel was an old white mailbox. Over the years the mailbox had become more rust colored than white. I noticed there were still no vehicle tracks in the main road or any coming from the drive I was about to enter. Turning into the driveway, I noticed the road here didn't seem as muddy as a few miles back.

When I had gone a few hundred feet, I could see the blue glare of the house vapor light glowing through the trees. There was just enough breeze to make the cool green oak tree leaves dance and turn in the dim blue light. When I approached the older white wood frame house at the end of the road, I noticed the outline of someone standing on the edge of the lighted area with his back toward me. He was facing away from the house looking down into the creek bottom below. It looked to me as though he was clinging to a partly deteriorated post barely supporting the barbed wire fence attached to it. I pulled my vehicle close to where the shadowy figure stood and stepped out of the truck.

"Did I get here in time, Mr. Crowe?" I asked.

"I knew all the rain on those roads would slow you down some," he said. "I got to thinking about that after I called and tried to call you back. Someone at your house said you were already gone though so I figured you would come out here to the house first. I wanted to get back with you and tell you it would probably be better if you took that old road over east because I think that's where they went out."

After Mr. Crowe said that, I felt my heart sink. I knew that with the bad road conditions, I probably wouldn't be able to catch up to the vehicle before it got to the main highway about three miles east of Mr. Crowe's house.

"You know, I am about sick and tired of all this trouble. I have posted my property at every corner and still can't seem to keep these guys off my land," Mr. Crowe exclaimed.

I felt very inadequate at Mr. Crowe's statement, knowing that the damage had already been done, and there was not a lot I could do after the fact, according to state laws. I asked Mr. Crowe if he had heard these guys shoot.

He said, "No, at first I just heard their dogs running and bellowing all up and down the creek. Then I heard the dogs bark like they had treed something. Then shortly after that I saw three separate lights, like flashlights, going through the woods over to where the dogs were treed. I guess they were chasing raccoons or something. It seems like this happens every year about this time. After I called you, I started to go down there myself and see what they were doing. Then I decided at my age that might not be too good an idea. Besides, when I got down there I would have gotten mad and

4

probably caused more problems than you and I could take care of because I was gonna take my shotgun."

I apologized to him and tried to explain what had taken me so long to get there. He nodded his head and said he understood. He said, "What I don't understand is why someone would be chasing raccoons this time of year. Ain't they got babies?"

"Yes, Sir," I said, "that's highly possible, because raccoons have their kittens in late April or early May."

"That's just what I thought," Mr. Crowe said. "I think these guys were trying to catch a pregnant female so they could get her and her kittens."

"Yes, Sir," I said. "It's not uncommon for these people to try and catch a pregnant female or even run her back to her den tree to try and get her or her babies."

"That must have been what I heard then," Mr. Crowe replied.

"What do you mean?" I asked.

"I could hear a chain saw running and then what sounded like someone chopping wood," Mr. Crowe said.

My attention suddenly perked up. I had received another report from a land owner in the southern part of my county about a week earlier on a similar complaint. Following up on the complaint revealed information that three brothers who owned a bar in the south end of my county had been cutting down raccoon den trees and taking the mothers and their kittens. They would take the raccoons to the bar on Saturday night and sell them for twenty dollars each to the other coon hound men in the surrounding counties. The hounds men would cage up the raccoons in small three foot cages and tease the dogs for sport. Sometimes the dogs would tear the cages apart and kill the raccoons. This was done under the pretense of training the dogs. Raccoon hunters usually trained their hound pups this way, specially so the pups could get a taste of blood. The old coon hunters said this made the pups grow up to be more fierce and want to kill when they attacked a raccoon.

Walking over closer to the fence, I looked down toward the hardwood bottom. Then I asked Mr. Crowe to point in the general direction of where he had seen the lights and heard the chopping noises. He pointed east over to the edge of the red bluff that his home was located on. He said, "Down there where the creek turns back north."

It was about fifty yards out in the flat among all the cottonwoods and bigger oak trees. He said, "If you want to you can climb over this fence and go around the edge of the hill until you get to the first pasture. Then all you need to do when you get there is just follow the creek, and it'll take you right over there."

I didn't want Mr. Crowe to be concerned, but I had walked these fields and pastures many nights alone chasing coon hunters and deer poachers. I was more familiar with this property than he knew. I returned to my truck, pulled my flashlight from the holder and walked back to the fence where Mr. Crowe was still standing.

I said, "Mr. Crowe, these guys are already gone, but I am gonna go down toward the creek and have a good look around that area anyway. I'm talking about looking around down in the area where you last saw the lights. If I happen to run across anything interesting, I'll get back with you."

He said, "Okay. If you need me, I'll be in the house. Just knock."

Climbing over the sagging, rusty fence, I began my walk to the creek bottom. The grass was still wet from the rain. I hadn't gone far when my boots became wet all the way through to my socks. I wasn't really concerned because I thought I would end up wading in the creek before the night was over anyway.

CHAPTER 2

The wind had become completely still. I stopped in the dark for a moment just to listen. I could hear the drops of rain falling from the leaves to the ground. The rain drops seemed to make more noise falling from the leaves up higher and hitting the leaves below than when the drops actually made it all the way to the ground. The spring peeper frogs were croaking. Sometimes the frogs would become so harmonious it sounded like singing. Then in one instant, the frogs would all quit singing, and it would be totally quiet. When this happened the only other sound would be from the water trickling in the creek. It hadn't rained enough earlier in the day to make the water in the creek have a definite rushing sound. I looked up toward the night sky and could see the thin, white, wispy clouds the storm had left behind. I could see the moon through the clouds and the blue glare was almost like the vapor light from Mr. Crowe's house. The natural glow of the moon's blue light seemed to have a calming effect on me even though the clouds and moon both seemed to be moving in opposite directions at the same time. There was not a sound except for the sounds of nature.

I managed to make it from the house, around the hill and across the pasture without ever turning on my flashlight. Just the blue moon's glow was more than a sufficient amount of light to move silently through the woods. When I arrived at the point where Mr. Crowe thought he had last seen and heard the hunters, I stopped again. Bending down on my knees with my feet tucked under my body, I was actually sitting on my heels with my knees firmly planted in the soft soil in front of me. From my years in the outdoors and from my military experience in Vietnam, I learned I could sit this way for an extended period of time and be completely comfortable and silent. After listening to the sounds for awhile, I decided to move again. After only a few yards, I detected a new scent in the air I had not smelled previously that day. The smell was very familiar to me because I had grown up in the woods with my Dad and helped him cut and stack many cords of firewood in my youth. There was no mistake about it; I could smell fresh cut wood or wet sawdust. I stood quietly for a few more seconds, then turned on my flashlight to have a better look around. There was less light in the area toward the creek. Since the small breeze that started earlier had changed directions, the creek area was where the smell of the freshly cut wood had to be coming from. I shined my flashlight back toward the creek.

I could see the top of a tree stump exposed to show fresh cut marks. It looked as if the tree had fallen toward the creek after being cut down. I moved closer and noticed that the tree was hollow inside and had partially broken open along the trunk upon impact with the ground. Small square chips of wood were lying around under the main part of the trunk. Part of the bottom of the tree managed to remain intact with the stump. About six feet up on the main part of the tree, someone had taken an ax and cut a small hole about one foot square into the tree's main trunk. I walked up to the open end of the tree's trunk; it was pointed in my direction. Then I shined my light back into the hollow hole along the split where it had broken open when it fell. It was then I noticed the first droplet of blood. I could see small patches and smears of blood along the top and inside of the log's hollow area. I could also see lots of hair. Most of it seemed to be dog hair; short, coarse and black. There were some brown hairs, shorter and finer like the hair of a dog's ear, but not as many. I climbed on top of the fallen tree, laid my body flat out on the downed tree and shined my light as far back into the cavity of the tree as I could. I couldn't see anything in the hollow except where a raccoon had built its nest.

The nest was made of dried leaves and grass with some bark from an elm tree that the mother chewed into small pieces to line her nest. Most mother raccoons line their nest with chewed bark so when the kittens are born, the bark will absorb the moisture from the birth, plus keep the mother's scent on the babies. The nest looked like a finely made Easter basket. It would be cozy, warm and always dry until the babies were old enough for the mother to take them out on their own. I pushed myself to an upright position, then clenched my legs firmly around the tree trunk. As I moved to my sitting position, I caught a new and very distinct odor that over the years had become too familiar. I reached for my flashlight and again started to shine it back toward the edge of the creek. It was then that my eyes caught what I was looking for, but didn't really want to find. I could see part of the fur and almost all the rings that made the circles on a raccoon's tail. I was looking at a small, motionless body, partly exposed through the grass that had grown up around another fallen log, partially decomposed by moisture and insects. It looked as though the log had fallen there from natural causes. The tree had probably reached maturity and died. The weather over the years had made the tree give up, fall over and start a new life cycle among the grass and plants where it lay.

I swung my leg over the log I was straddling and slowly slid off the log to the moist ground below. The distinctive smell I noticed was from the blood and scent of the raccoon's body that lay limp on the ground. The scent was from the courageous flight the mother raccoon had made against the pack of dogs while trying to protect her babies. I walked closer and could see from the evidence of large paw prints that there could have been no less than four of these large hounds. It was also evident by the stench in the air that I truly could smell death. Sheer numbers alone, plus the help of the poachers, had caused the mother's untimely death. Alongside her body was a long sharpened stick the poachers had used to twist and punch the mother raccoon from her hollow snag. Then I realized from remembering the blood droplets and hair from inside the hollow log exactly what had happened.

The poachers had chased the mother raccoon back to her den and nesting area. Taking a chain saw, they cut down the tree to try and gain access to the mother. When the tree fell, it shattered and broke her nest loose from the inside of the walls of her hollow sanctuary. She obviously had made a very gallant and courageous stand against her enemies. She somehow managed back herself into the hollow cavity of the downed tree where no enemies could gain access from behind her, except man. There was only room at the front entrance to the log for one dog at a time. The blood droplets and hair were from the dogs' faces and ears where the mother raccoon had made her final effort to protect what mattered most to her, her babies.

She tried to defend herself and her kittens from the dogs by attacking the dogs when one of the hounds would enter her hollow domain. The poachers could see from the mother's persistence that it was going to take human intervention to dislodge her from her home. The poachers took an ax and chopped a hole into the fallen tree just behind where the mother had taken her stand. By chopping the hole in the upper trunk of the tree, the poachers had gained access to where the mother was located. Then the poachers took a long willow stick and sharpened it at one end. They placed the sharp end of the stick into the hollow cavity and pushed it forward toward where the mother was located. From the small patches of fur found alongside the sharpened stick, it was evident that the poachers not only poked the sharp end of the willow stick into her soft body but had managed to twist her silken fur around the end of the sharp stick. This had given them enough momentum to move her body forward so that one of the hounds could bury his teeth into her body and pull her from the log.

Once pulled outside the log, it was very evident she was no match for hounds and men. The hounds had ripped and torn most of the skin off her body. Her fur was almost totally soaked in blood from the tip of her nose to her shiny black ringed tail. There was a deep open gash-like wound across her neck area where one of the hounds finally managed to get his powerful death grip on her small throat, crushing it and finally suffocating her, while the other hounds tore at her lifeless body. Small lines of white trickled from her breast. It was the life giving milk needed to support her kittens. My stomach felt queasy and I became both angry and emotionally upset at the same time. I thought to myself, "What kind of person could maim and kill such a beautiful animal in the name of sportsmanship, or for the mere amount of money they would receive for her kittens?" I told myself that no matter what the hounds men call it, to me it was a cruel and senseless murder!

I walked away from the mother's body a few yards and found a fairly large stick. I went to the edge of the clearing and knelt down forward on my knees and started to dig. The more I let my mind wonder over what I had just seen, the more deliberate my blows became into the soft sand where I was digging. At one point I quit digging to stop and listen to nature's quieting sounds once again. The sounds were the same, but everything seemed different after witnessing the brutal sight. I finished digging the hole, which was about two feet side, two feet long and two feet deep. Then I went back beyond the tree and retrieved the mother raccoon from where she had died. I carried her limp body over to the hole and gently laid her inside. I stared quietly at her lifeless shadowy outline in the moonlight and then took my bare hands and covered her up. After rounding and packing the dirt on her grave, I stood and with the back of my muddy hand wiped a single tear that was trying to roll down my cheek. Then I turned and headed for the creek. My walk had quickened to almost a jog. Reaching the creek, I bent down and submerged my hands in the water as deep as I could reach without falling forward into the pool. I felt as if I had been part of a great sin against God and nature. I needed to wash all the evidence from my hands.

While I was sitting with my head drooped and hands extended into the water, I heard a completely different noise. I immediately pulled my hands from the water, stood and focused my attention to the sound. I couldn't course the direction of the sound, so I climbed to the top of the creek bank and wiped the water from my hands onto my pants' leg. I then cupped each hand behind my ears to amplify the sound I was hearing. I couldn't tell at first if the sound was just muffled or a long way off. I kept turning my head from left to right trying to course the sound and maybe identify exactly what I was hearing. Walking a few yards forward, I cupped my ears and listened again. This time I knew the sound was close but didn't know exactly where it was coming from. After waiting and listening a few minutes, I never heard the sound again.

I walked back toward where I had buried the mother raccoon. On the way, I stopped and cut a small limb from a young native elm that had sprouted and grown up under the canopy of the larger trees. At the grave site, I sat down cross-legged and started to peel the bark from the elm branch. After cleaning and scraping a section of branch about three feet long, I took my knife and cut the cleaned branch into two sections, one piece about two feet long and one piece about a foot long. I retrieved a short strand of the elm bark that I had peeled off the branch from the ground. Then I thought it would probably be more fitting if I used a piece of bark from the nest the mother had made for her babies. I returned to the hollow tree to spot where the poachers had chopped the hole in the main trunk. Leaning over, and placing my arm in the dark hole, I felt around until I found the center portion of her nest. As I was pulling a long strand of elm bark from the nest, I thought how ironic it was that the inside portion of the nest was still warm. Then I took the strand of bark that the mother had peeled and chewed and tied the two limbs I had cut together. In the moonlight the white of the fresh peeled branches made a perfect cross.

After taking no more than a couple of long steps away from the fallen log, I heard the peculiar sound again. Whatever was making the sound had to be close by. I stopped and turned back toward the fallen tree where I had just gotten the chewed strand of bark. At first I thought it was the chirping made my sand crickets. Then it became louder, and I felt the blood rush through my body. It was the weak chattering sound of a baby raccoon. I exploded with excitement!

I grabbed my flashlight, jumped on top of the log and began looking in every direction inside of the hollow tree. The hole the poachers had made was small, but I could still see part of the mother raccoon's nest inside. I thought to myself that it was possible when the hollow tree fell, the concussion of the fall had jarred one of the kittens from the nest. Maybe in their hurried frenzy to grab the baby raccoons and run, the poachers missed a kitten and left it behind. Looking in both directions inside the log using my flashlight, I could detect no movement whatsoever. So I hurried to the larger, open end of the log and flashed my light as deeply into the long hollow tree cavity as my light would shine. All I could see were parts of the nest scattered along the bottom of the open hole. I quickly returned to the open hole the poachers had made. I placed my head close to the open hole and listened intently for any sound. Wishing for a chirp or chatter, all I heard was the barely visible sound of leaves rustling. I thrust my arm as far as I could reach into the open hole and began digging through the leaves and main parts of the mother raccoon's nest. Suddenly I felt the unmistakable long hind foot of a baby raccoon. I grasped it firmly, yet gently, and gave it a tug, feeling the hot, wrinkly body of the baby raccoon. I pulled it from the nest and cupped it into the palm of both my hands. The baby raccoon could not have been more than eight inches long, tail and all. I was concerned how small the baby raccoon was and knew I needed to move fast if there would be any chance at all of saving its life. I jumped from the log, picked up my cross from off the ground and ran back to the mother's grave site. I stuck the elm cross at the head of the mother's grave. Then I said, "I've got one of your babies, and I'm going to try and save it."

For the kitten to be safe, I would need to keep it warm until I made my way back to my truck. I took off my long sleeved outer shirt and pulled my T-shirt over my head. The cool night air made the hair on my body stand on end. I quickly took the kitten and placed it inside my cotton T-shirt and wrapped the shirt loosely around the small raccoon's body. I then placed my outer shirt back on, tucking the long tails of the shirt inside my jeans. Immediately, I placed the baby inside my shirt close to my body so my body heat would transfer to the baby and keep it warm. Then, I broke into a slow trot back toward my truck. I looked back over my shoulder, as I started my trot; I could still see the white elm cross on the mother's grave shining in the moonlight.

CHAPTER 3

I thought to myself that 3:00 in the morning would not be a good time to start searching for everything I would need to start raising a baby raccoon. I had dealt with many small animals before because of my career in Wildlife Law Enforcement. I gained a lot of experience over the years by picking up numerous types of animals from farmers and ranchers in the area. Most of the orphans I was called to pick up were baby fawn deer. These fawns were usually found by the landowners moving hay or cutting grain fields with large pieces of machinery. The loud metal clattering noises would scare the baby deer and they would jump and run from their secluded hiding places where their mothers had placed them for protection. Then, after finishing work in their fields, the farmers or ranchers would go back and catch the fawn deer, thinking that since the baby fawns had been disturbed, the mother deer would not be able to find them and to feed and care for them. I kept trying to convince the farmers and ranchers that this was far from the truth, and that all baby wildlife would be better off if left alone. Yet, every year I received calls to come and pick up three or four baby fawns that had become "lost." Tending to the baby deer was fairly easy though. All I needed to do was get a large baby bottle, fill it with milk and feed the fawns three or four times a day. The fawns would start growing fast. After a few months, the fawns would be capable of making it on their own and would be turned back into the wild.

Caring for baby birds I had found was a little different and turned out to be a lot more confining and time consuming than I ever thought it would be. It was extremely difficult to come up with, let's say, ten mice per day to feed a baby hawk or a pair of baby barn owls. I tried my hand at feeding four baby Monkey Faced Owls a rancher brought to me. He found the baby owls while tearing down an old, abandoned farm house on some of his property. All I could remember about the baby owls was that they screeched all day and all night, and that every time I looked at the baby owls they had their mouths open wanting to be fed. The day I released the barn owls back into the wild, I felt a great sense of relief. It was as if a heavy burden had been lifted from my shoulders.

After my experience with the owls, I managed to talk a retired junior high school teacher into getting involved with wildlife and becoming a licensed wildlife rehabilitator. She applied for and received all the federal permits required to care for all species of birds from common song birds to birds of prey such as hawks, owls and eagles. Her favorites seemed to be hawks and owls. Over the years, she fed back to life or retrained hundreds of birds of every kind and released them back into the wild. What made her so efficient at her job was that she had an outside source for food that no one else had. Her husband worked in one of the local grain elevators and had access to more mice than one could imagine. He would always go out of his way to keep his live traps set in the granaries so he could provide the mice needed to feed his wife's abandoned or wounded birds.

One other thing I learned through my personal experience with raising baby animals was that baby fawn deer needed to have a special bacterium to digest food. Without this cultured milk and bacteria from its mother in its stomach, a baby fawn would literally starve to death no matter how much or what it ate. The only place to get the bacteria was from the first few gulps of raw milk a fawn received from its mother's milk sac. I looked over in the seat of my truck at the small bundle wrapped in my white T-shirt and wondered if baby raccoons needed the same bacteria and cultured milk that fawns needed, and if so, had the baby raccoon been alive long enough to receive this life saving milk. I remembered the lines of milk on the dead mother raccoon's breast and simply hoped for the best.

Going directly to the main highway, I was taking the longer route home hoping to save time. This way I avoided going back over the miles of muddy roads taken to get to Mr. Crowe's house. It was almost 4:00 a.m. by the time I made it home. When I reached my house, I leaned over in the seat of my truck and gently picked up the white bundle. The warmth of the baby raccoon's body could be felt through the shirt. I carried the small bundle into the house and softly set it down in the fold along the arm of the reclining chair.

I went to the phone and immediately started dialing the veterinarian. Cathy Britte was a long time friend of mine and she had always shown a great desire to assist me in any of my wildlife rehabilitation projects. Once, I had taken her an immature bald eagle that had been shot with a small caliber rifle. The shot shattered the eagle's right wing bone. Along with the help of two electric line workers who had found the eagle, I managed to get the eagle subdued and wrapped it inside a cut up burlap sack. This kept the eagle's wings pinned to its side so as not to do any more damage to is wings while transporting it to the veterinarian. Cathy performed a major four hour operation on the eagle replacing splintered bone with metal and screws. The operation was a complete success, and after a few months of rehabilitation by the retired teacher, the eagle was released back into the wild. This eagle, that I once held in my hands, was later spotted in the Bob Marshall Wilderness Area in western Montana by US Fish and Wildlife Biologist. This rewarding news made my life seem worthwhile.

When I heard the phone click on the other end of the line as if someone had picked up the receiver, I said, "Hello, Cathy. This is State Game Warden Dekota Cagle. I'm sorry to be calling you this time of the night. In case you haven't looked at your clock, it's four in the morning. I really hate to call and trouble you with this, but I need some expert veterinary advice. Earlier tonight I rescued a baby raccoon from its nest inside a den tree that had been cut down by poachers. I found that the poachers had killed the mother and stole the rest of her kittens. In the poachers' haste to leave, they must have overlooked one kitten, and I managed to find and retrieve it. I want to try and raise it until it's big enough to be released back into the wild."

I sounded like Cathy was yawning and trying to gather her senses on the other end of the phone line.

"How big is it?" she asked.

21

"It's very small," I said. "There is barely any hair visible on its body. I guess it couldn't be over five days old because its eyes are still closed."

Her voice cracked as she said, "That doesn't sound good at all. Usually a kitten that small doesn't make it."

I quickly interrupted her and said, "I'll do anything necessary to try and save the baby raccoon's life." I knew that at the mother's grave site I had made a solemn vow to do everything I could to see that her baby lived.

Cathy assured me, "If the kitten is in sound shape and not injured from the jolt of the den tree falling, it should be fine for six to eight hours before it will run into any kind of real trouble." Cathy continued, "Bring it in to the office as soon as you can tomorrow morning, and I'll have a look at it."

I replied, "That will be my first priority tomorrow morning as soon as my feet hit the floor." Again I apologized for the time of my call and hung up the phone.

Opening the hall closet, I looked along the top shelf until I saw a shoe box that I thought would make a good bed for the kitten. Then I went into the utility room and searched until I found some old dish towels. During my search I found some cotton lining that had been pressed flat as if it had been used to line a separate box that had been filled with glasses or something very fragile. I took all my collected materials and returned to the recliner where I had left the small, white bundle. I unwrapped the baby raccoon from my T-shirt and held its small, trembling body in my hands. Then I softly made a small cavity down into the soft cotton with my fist and ever so gently placed the baby inside its new bed. The kitten made a weak chattering sound when I placed it inside. The kitten crawled in a complete circle nudging into the cotton lining along the sides of the box. It was as if it were searching for one of its brothers or sisters to snuggle up against. It curled its body up into a tiny pinkish-gray ball and became perfectly still. It looked at peace. I set the box in back of the recliner next to the wall and close to the heating vent where I knew it would be safe and warm until tomorrow morning.

I walked quietly back to the bedroom and sat on the edge of my bed. Pulling my boots off, I realized they were still wet from my trip through the woods and damp grass.

As quietly as possible, I eased into bed trying not to wake my wife. When I crawled beneath the blankets, I realized I had company. Some time during my absence in the night, my seven-year old daughter had made her way into a safer, warmer spot next to her mother. As I settled down to try and sleep, my daughter rolled and faced me. Eventually when she stopped moving, she had managed to snuggle her head up on my extended arm with her cheek lying against my chest. I reached down, kissed her forehead and finally drifted off to sleep.

CHAPTER 4

The next morning I was up early. Looking out my bedroom window, I could see the glistening and sparkle of sunlight on the grass from the heavy dew left from the night before. Walking to the front room, I retrieved the shoe box from behind the recliner. I slowly peeled the layers of cotton back until the body of the baby raccoon was revealed. Gently scooping my hand under the small, gray ball I had uncovered, the baby nuzzled around in the palm of my hand as if it were looking for a nipple to suck. For the first time since I had plucked it from the hollow log, I was getting a good look at its tiny body.

Its body was a light gray color with very little hair. The hair on its body was so thin, in fact, you could see its pink, wrinkly skin underneath. The only hair of any length at all was on its tail. There, you could see the faint markings of where the rings on its tail would later be. I examined it very closely looking for any sign of injury. The only distinct marking on its whole body was a small patch of light colored hair at the base of its lower jaw and throat. During my examination, I discovered it was a female. Unconsciously, I compared it to other baby raccoons I had seen, and because of its frail size, I thought it might have been the runt of the litter. As I cupped it in both hands, I thought of when I was trying to save it from the hollow tree. My mental image had been of a soft, warm furry and cuddly baby raccoon. In real life and with plenty of light available, it was actually ugly.

The rest of my family was stirring in the back bedroom. My wife was helping our daughter get ready for school. I returned the box to its original location behind the chair and sat down to put my other boot on so I could get ready to take the baby raccoon to town to the veterinarian. As I finished tying my last boot lace on my second boot, I heard tiny, sock-covered feet thumping on the hard wooden floor as they made their way down the hallway to where I sat.

"Good morning Punkin," I said as my daughter made her way across the room and jumped into my lap. "Are you about ready for school to be out?"

"I guess," she said.

"Well, you only have one more month and then you'll be out of school for the rest of the summer," I said.

Punkin climbed from my lap and had begun to put her shoes on when she said, "What I like most about summer is getting to go swimming."

While she was working trying to tie her shoe laces, I made my way to the back of the recliner and picked up the shoe box. I returned to the couch and sat down next to her. "Guess what I found last night?" I asked Punkin.

Punkin then glanced over at the shoe box in my hands with very little interest and said, "I don't know. What?"

"A baby raccoon," I said.

Suddenly her face lit up as she scooted closer to me. "Is it in the box?" she asked.

"Yes," I said, "Do you want to have a look?"

"Oh, Daddy, it's so tiny," she said. "Can I have it, Daddy?"

"Well, Punkin, you can't really own something wild, but I thought maybe you and I could try raising it," I explained.

I could see a sparkle deep in her blue-green eyes as she stared at the baby. She slowly reached into the box and softly ran a single finger across the baby's body. "Is it a boy or a girl, Daddy?" she asked.

"It's a girl, Honey." I said.

"Can I name it?" she asked.

"Sure, what would you like to call it?" I said.

Punkin replied, "I don't know yet, but I'll think about it."

As she finished getting dressed for school, I returned the box to its place behind the chair. A few minutes later as I walked away from the large bay windows in the front of the house, I said, "You better get out there; the bus is coming."

Punkin gulped her last swallow of milk and ran toward me. I bent over at the waist to meet her, knowing she had come for her good-bye kiss. "Bye, Punkin," I said.

"By, Daddy." She said, "I love you."

Then out the door and down the wooden steps she ran. I walked to the picture window and watched as she ran down the driveway to meet the bus. Her long, golden hair bounced and swayed in the oncoming wind even though her mother had tied it snugly with rubber bands into two long pony-tails.

CHAPTER 5

The gravel was popping under my tires as I pulled up to the front of the veterinarian clinic. I reached over onto the seat of my truck and picked up the box that held the tiny survivor from the night before. As I stepped out of my truck, Cathy was already holding the door open to her clinic. I guessed that she had either seen or heard me drive up. I entered the office and was escorted to a back room that resembled a hospital emergency room. I set my box on a long, gray examination table, turned and looked at Cathy who walked into the room behind me.

Without saying a word, she opened the box and lifted out the baby raccoon. She seemed to start at the tip of the raccoon's nose and ended her examination at the black tip of its tail.

"I don't think it's hurt, but you're going to have your hands full trying to save a raccoon this small," she said. "You will need to feed it every two or three hours for the first couple of weeks."

That statement concerned me because I was on call 24 hours a day, and I could be called out and be gone away from home for extended periods of time. I explained to Cathy, "I'll do my best. In about one month my daughter will be out of school and able to help with the responsibilities of feeding."

Cathy escorted me to the back of the clinic through a long, dark hallway. Halfway down the hallway, I could see through an opening to my left. Through the opening, all I could see were the pens that held the other animals brought to Cathy to be cared for.

"Do you still have the cougar we confiscated?" I asked.

"Yes," she replied, "and both the wolves."

Cathy had stopped in front of a large, metal cabinet and was shuffling glass bottles from one shelf to the next. Finally, Cathy turned around and handed me a pint sized glass bottle and said, "This bottle contains condensed milk that is used to feed malnourished baby kittens. It has everything the baby raccoon will need to survive. The milk in this bottle has all the nutrients needed to get the baby raccoon off to a healthy start."

She pulled open a lower drawer from the cabinet and retrieved two small milk bottles. These small bottles looked exactly like human baby bottles. Each bottle was about one inch in diameter and about three inches long. She made a small incision in the tip of each nipple to be sure enough milk was passing through the tip when the baby fed.

Cathy made a gesture by pointing to the side of the bottle.

"The first couple of days, feed quality not quantity. You'll need to feed at least once every hour in small doses until the baby gets acclimated to its new food source. I would even recommend using these for the first couple of days," Cathy advised.

In her left hand, she held what appeared to be an eye dropper or one of the long plastic droppers I had seen used to give Punkin her first vitamins when she was a baby. I gathered all my supplies and my box and headed for the front desk. After setting all my packages on the counter, I made out a check for the milk and bottles.

"You said you still have the cougar and the two wolves I brought you?" I said.

"Yes," she said, "they're in the larger pens out back."

"How are they doing?" I asked.

"Much better than when you brought them to me. The cougar was in such poor condition, I almost lost it," she said.

I asked, "Could I go to the pens and see them?"

"Sure," she said, "help yourself."

I walked the long, dark hall until I reached the very back of the metal building. I approached the first cage and in the far corner sat the half grown female cougar. Her body still revealed the abusive treatment she had received from her previous owner. Less than one month earlier, I had confiscated the cougar and two wolves from a commercial game breeder. All three animals had almost been starved to death. The owner made no effort to properly feed or care for the animals. When I arrived at the owner's residence to confiscate the animals, the only food available to these animals was dead chicken carcasses retrieved from a creek bed where they were being dumped by local people who owned commercial chicken houses. The wolves and cougar were forced to live in their own filth because the owner failed to clean their cages. As I now stood and looked at the cougar, I could see the effect such treatment had on her sleek body. I could still see her rib cage through her dark tan skin and a ridge down her back from her back bones that were visible underneath her skin. She had lost all the hair from around the tops of her feet from a fungus she acquired from walking in her own filth while caged. The female cougar sat and stared at me. I could see in her dark yellow-brown eyes that if it were possible, she would take her revenge for being caged out on me. Although I had actually been her savior, her heart told her I was "man" and was totally responsible for her being caged.

I walked to the cage that held the two wolves. Both wolves paced back and forth from side to side in their 12 foot by 12 foot cage, all the while never breaking eye contact with me. The wolves' deep yellow-gray eyes seemed to be able to look inside my soul. The glare in their eyes seemed to say, "Look around at the animals in these cages. You humans have sentenced us to a life in prison for a crime we never committed. All we ever wanted was our God given right to live free." At that moment I could feel guilt and a compassion for animals I had never felt before. I heard my own conscience vow that I would never chain or cage a wild animal or interfere with its right to be free again.

I walked back to the front of the clinic, picked up my bottles, the brown paper sack which contained the milk, and my box with the baby raccoon inside. Without saying a word, I walked out to my truck.

CHAPTER 6

I set one of the bottles of milk into a pan of water on the stove. I was making every effort to warm the baby's milk, yet not get it too hot. After testing the milk on my wrist a few times, I was satisfied the milk was body temperature. Digging into the bottom of my paper sack, I found the plastic eye dropper. I took the milk, eye dropper, and baby to the couch. I filled the eye dropper with milk and prepared to give the baby its first taste of cat's milk. Softly I gripped my hand around the upper body of the baby and placed the eye dropper into the curl of its pink extended tongue. At first it licked at the milk a couple of times. Then it began to paw upward at the eye dropper as if it needed something to press its tiny front feet against while it fed. It never actually sucked on the dropper as I had expected. I thought maybe if I squeezed the black tip on the dropper, it would force more milk into the baby raccoon's mouth. I squeezed the dropper and forced too much milk into its mouth. The kitten suddenly became strangled. It began to cough and spew milk from its nostrils while gasping for air. The milk coming from its nose was making tiny white bubbles around its mouth. These tiny milk bubbles looked almost like soap bubbles. I turned the baby over on its stomach and let it catch its breath. After a couple of minutes, I picked up a small washcloth from out of the shoe box and wrapped it around the whole body of the baby. I then returned to the licking method of feeding, with the baby sitting more in an upright position. This seemed more effective, but it didn't look like the baby was getting a lot of milk. Then I realized what the veterinarian had meant. Because of the size of the baby, its stomach could not hold a full eye dropper of milk.

I stayed home the rest of the day feeding the kitten about one half eye dropper full every hour.

My wife came home from work, and I explained what my intentions were with the baby raccoon. I told her, "Punkin and I will assume most of the responsibilities for trying to raise the baby raccoon, but in all reality it will probably become a family affair."

Glancing at the clock, I noticed it was time for the bus to be making its afternoon rounds. It Would soon be stopping to let Punkin off at home. The thought had no more than cleared my mind when I could hear the whine of the mud-gripped tires of the bus on the black asphalt road in front of the house. I walked to the front door just in time to see Punkin come dashing from the opposite side of the bus. She was running with her head tilted back and her thin arms pumping up and down as if she was running for a real purpose. Although it was only fifty yards from the road to the house, her pace slowed to a fast walk by the time she reached the porch.

Gasping between breaths as she entered the house, she ran straight to where I stood and asked, "Where's the baby raccoon?"

I told her, "It's asleep in the shoe box at the moment, but it will need to be fed before very long."

"How long, Daddy?" she asked.

"By the time you put away your books and change clothes, it will probably be time," I said.

She whizzed off in the opposite direction toward her bedroom. I could hear her rummaging around, sliding dresser drawers in and out, looking for clothes other than her good school clothes.

I had already started to warm a small amount of milk knowing I would receive no peace until she at least got to hold the baby. When she had returned from her room, we both went in and sat on the couch. I explained what the veterinarian told me about how often and what amounts of milk we would need to feed the baby and that the baby would probably need to stay in the house for awhile until it could be sent outside and turned loose.

All the while I was explaining what needed to be done, I had the feeling that none of the real facts were sinking in to Punkin's thoughts. The total time I had been talking, her eyes were glued upon the box. The only other time I had seen such anticipation from her was on Christmas Eve. The gaze she held on the box was like a Christmas morning present that she was about to open.

I checked the milk, and it was ready. I picked up the eye-dropper and fresh wash cloth and said, "Punkin, go get the box and bring it to me."

She had the box and was standing before me in one split second. I took the box from her and told her to take a seat on the couch. Taking the baby from its box, I showed her exactly how to hold it. Then I taught her how to feed it by letting it lick the eye-dropper so it would not become strangled on the milk. Punkin had held baby kittens that had been born in the old milk barn at her Grandma's house. Until this very moment, I had never seen the tenderness Punkin was showing to the baby raccoon. It was almost mother-like. Punkin accomplished the whole chore of feeding the baby by herself. She cleaned and washed the dried milk from the baby's face once it was finished eating and gave its nose a little kiss before putting it back into its box. Punkin had done everything.

After the feeding, Punkin came and sat down in my lap. She reached up and locked her arms around my neck and quietly whispered, "Thank you, Daddy, for getting my raccoon."

I said, "You're welcome, Honey. Just remember that baby raccoon is a wild animal and you can't really own a wild raccoon. Someday we will need to set it free."

All at once I realized that maybe she hadn't heard what I said earlier. She gave me a long, hard look directly into my eyes and without saying a word, I could sense she was thinking, "Daddy, you wouldn't take that baby raccoon away from me."

After sitting on my lap for a few minutes and starring at the box as if in meditation, Punkin turned to me and said, "Daddy, you said I could name the raccoon, right?"

"Sure," I said, "what would you like to call her?"

"I want to call her Sally," she said, "and she can have a middle name like mine too, Ann."

I said, "Sally Ann. Now that's a name to remember."

I set Punkin down off my lap, stood up, and started to the kitchen to put away the rest of Sally's milk. Punkin had gone directly to Sally's box and was starring intently into the soft cotton.

"Daddy," she asked, "where did you find Sally?"

That was a question I would answer but really wanted to avoid.

"I found Sally out by Mr. Crowe's house along the creek." I said.

"Was she lost?" Punkin asked.

I seemed to be getting deeper into the "question and answer scheme" than I actually wanted to.

I said, "Well, Sally was kind of lost and abandoned." Already I was trying to think of an answer to what I was afraid would be the next question.

"Daddy, where is Sally's Momma?" she asked.

I stopped what I was doing and walked around the end of the kitchen counter. Reaching down, I took Punkin's hand and led her over to the couch. I sat down and took both of Punkin's hands into mine. We were eye to eye, and she was standing straight up between my knees.

I said, "Honey, you do know what my job is as a Game Warden, don't you?"

She said, "Yes. You put the bad guys in jail for killing the animals."

I said, "Well, Punkin, you're partially right. I do put people in jail sometimes for killing deer, turkeys, or raccoons out of season. You see last night some men took their hounds and chased Sally's mother back to the tree where she had Sally and the rest of her kittens hid. These poachers then cut the tree down where Sally lived and let their hounds kill Sally's mother. Then they took Sally's brothers and sisters with them. They were probably going to sell or trade the other kittens to some other hunters."

After a long pause, she looked at me and said, "Why would anybody want to kill Sally's mother?"

"I don't know, Punkin. For money maybe or maybe no one ever taught them anything different," I replied. My thoughts raced back to the spot where I had gotten Sally and the gruesome scene it imbedded in my mind.

"I really don't know why someone would do that, Honey," I said again.

CHAPTER 7

Over the next few weeks, it became very time consuming to care for Sally. She had grown very quickly and had finally begun to grow hair over all of her body. Sally's little tail now had the definite markings of black rings like those on a mature raccoon's tail, and had the darker markings of the bandit's mask across her face and around her eyes. Her eyes had opened, and she had the most beautiful ebony eyes. They were like black, shiny pools of oil. Her eyes were always moist and glittered as if they were liquid. Sally had graduated from feeding from the eye-dropper to the small baby milk bottles. Her feedings were now about every four hours and everyone enjoyed their sleep.

School was out and Punkin spent most of her time playing with Sally. She carried Sally everywhere she went.

Sally would purr and chatter if placed in her box. She would act as though she had been abandoned and wanted attention from someone every minute of the day. It was almost like getting a baby used to sleeping in its own crib. When Sally's midnight feeding was over and we placed her back into her box, she would cry and chatter until she put herself to sleep.

During the day, Punkin did most of the feeding. She would hold Sally while she rocked her in the rocking chair. After feeding, Sally would curl up in a fetal position and go to sleep in Punkin's lap. They had become dependent on one another.

We all became very attached to Sally and ignored most of her troublesome antics. It wasn't uncommon for her to get on the back of the chair and dig in our hair ad though she was looking for fleas or maybe ticks. I laughed aloud many nights while Sally and Punkin rolled on the floor. Sally would sometimes act like a bear, lay back her ears, stand on her hind legs, and growl while lunging forward and diving into all the golden curls of hair on Punkin's head. Punkin would scream, laugh, and roll away, and Sally would attack again. This would go on nightly until they would finally wear each other out physically and end up curled together on the couch fast asleep.

Every spring our family planted a garden out along the creek just north of the big house. Everyone enjoyed our evenings working in the garden, especially Sally and Punkin. Their anticipation in the activity of gardening was actually more play than work, but both of them loved being outdoors. When the corn was about knee-high, Sally would run the rows and play hide and seek with Punkin. Sally would hike in the corn rows and whenever anyone walked down between the rows where Sally was hidden, she would attack their feet. Sometimes she would be so rambunctious during these attacks that we would have to give her a little swat to make her quit. We usually watered our garden by running a long, green garden hose from the big house out to the end of the garden. Then we would make small furrows between the rows with the pointed edge of a garden hoe. Since the lay of the land was slightly downhill toward the creek bed, all we had to do was turn the water on at a slow trickle and slowly flood the small ditches between each row. Sally loved this because it was her first contact with running water. It actually initiated her to the way a normal raccoon would get its food; in and around water. Sally would roll, dig and play in the small trickling stream produced by the hose.

The fresh running water brought the smell of the freshly hoed dirt alive. It was as if one could actually smell the reason seeds sprouted and grew in our warm, moist Oklahoma soil. Sally very seldom ventured far from where Punkin was on our evening trips to the garden. Even though Sally liked sneaking out alone among the corn rows, she would chatter an "I am lost" call if she was out of our sight very long. Sally was not a very independent raccoon. Of course, when Sally made her lost calls, Punkin would immediately seek her out and pick her up, no matter how mud-covered or water-soaked Sally might be. Then all would be well or at least until Sally became lost again.

While Punkin and Sally were playing the corn rows one day, Punkin made a discovery. Punkin yelled at me because I was at the far end of the corn row.

"Daddy, come look at this," Punkin yelled.

I hoed weeds back to the end of the row that Punkin and Sally were playing on, near to where the hose was trickling water.

"Look, Daddy," she said. Then Punkin pointed to a small hand print she had made in a large mud pie. Off to one side of where she was sitting were a couple more small mud pies.

"Now watch this!" she exclaimed.

She picked up Sally and took her right-front paw and made a perfect raccoon track in one of the mud pies. It was if Punkin were a kindergarten teacher helping one of her students make a perfect hand print in plaster of paris, which would later turn out to be a very special Christmas gift for the child's mother.

Punkin pointed to the small paw print and said, "Look, Daddy, Sally has hands just like mine." Then Punkin turned Sally over on her back and intently looked at the soft bottoms of Sally's hind-feet and front paws.

"Why doesn't Sally get stickers?" Punkin asked.

"Well, Honey, she does sometimes. You know when Sally nibbles at the bottom of her feet? Well, that's when she has a sand bur, and the only way she can get it out is with her teeth," I replied. The muscles around Punkin's eyes tightened up as if she were feeling the pain of Sally stepping on a sand bur.

"Daddy, I would pull the stickers out of Sally's feet," Punkin said sadly.

"I know, Honey," I said.

Then I went back to hoeing. The girls went back to making mud pies. Turning away from Punkin and Sally, as I hoed going away from them, my thoughts were that Punkin would not always be there to take Sally's pain or to pluck the sand burs from the bottoms of Sally's soft feet.

CHAPTER 8

One day I was home alone with Sally, working on my daily reports when I received a call from our county Sheriff's office. After my phone conversation with the Sheriff's office dispatcher, I determined I needed to leave immediately on this call. The only real problem was that I would need to leave Sally home alone. I picked up Sally and carried her into the bathroom to lock her up. She had become too much trouble to leave alone to roam the whole house. She would leave no cabinet door untouched or any boxes unopened, no matter what the contents. This had become quite a topic between Punkin, her mother and me.

Since I was in a rush, I thought there couldn't be a whole lot of trouble Sally could get into while locked in the bathroom. I found out differently when I returned home after being out on call. I had not yet fully opened the door to enter the big house when I was full faced by Punkin.

"Mom's mad at you," she said.

"Why?" I answered quickly.

"Because you left Sally in the bathroom all day," Punkin replied.

Suddenly I remembered it had been over four hours since I had been called out, and Sally had been locked in the bathroom all that time. Slowly I walked the hall back to where the bathroom door was located. I could distinguish a slight color change in the carpet under the bathroom door meaning that the carpet had become water soaked. While under the watchful eye of Punkin,

I opened the door slowly. I could not believe what I was seeing. I was astonished that a four pound raccoon could be so destructive. There was not a square inch inside of the small bathroom that did not have a glob of wet toilet paper stuck to it or smear marks of toothpaste covered paws. Somehow during my absence, Sally had managed to get inside the cabinet and gain access to about ten rolls of toilet tissue plus wash clothes and hand towels. She had chewed all the tubes of toothpaste into tiny metal strips. She had chewed wash cloths and hand towels into small trips for bedding. The worst part was she somehow managed to get the water in both the sink and the bathtub turned on. There were thousands of tiny hand prints on every wall but mostly on the mirror where it looked as if she were trying to apply make-up to herself. Her once pretty silken fur was now matted with toothpaste and small pieces of wet tissue.

I cautiously opened the door fully to be greeted by Sally still sitting in about two inches of water and what looked like paper mache that was still floating in the tub. I starred at Sally with squinted eyes and a look of contempt on my face. In return, I was greeted with a full grin and a loud chatter as if she were really glad to see me. Sally was sitting upright in the tub and playing with a blue plastic soap dish. I had once considered that particular soap dish to be out of the reach of most kids, but Sally had somehow managed to get to it. She looked quite content sitting there. It was if Sally had discovered her own personal play pen, and she loved it.

Slowly pulling the door shut, I looked at Punkin and said, "We're going to have to build Sally a house outside. She's getting much too big to stay in the house all the time."

After changing clothes, I went back into the bathroom and retrieved Sally from her playpen. I placed Sally on the floor, cleaned out the bathtub and finished giving Sally a real bath and shampoo. When I started her bath, I was a little upset with her, but she was so affectionate it was hard to stay mad at her. After hot baths, Sally always loved to be fluffed with the towel to dry her off. I had finished drying her off when she rolled over on her back in my hands and extended her long arms out and touched my face. The bottoms of her paws were soft and tender, almost like the bottoms of babies' feet, and her tender paws felt cool to the touch when she rubbed them along my face and cheeks. I pulled her close and nuzzled into the fur on her neck. She chattered like she knew she had already been forgiven. Then I bent down and set Sally in the hallway. She scurried off toward the back room where Punkin was playing.

I spent the next couple of hours cleaning up the bathroom. Occasionally during my chore, I would hear Punkin laugh and scream and could hear Sally chattering and growling. If I peeked from around the bathroom door, I would catch glimpses of Punkin and Sally as they dashed from one side of Punkin's bedroom to the other. I guess everyone had forgiven her!

Everyone got up early the following morning. Punkin seemed to be excited by the idea of our building Sally a house. There was already a place to start when we decided to get to our project. About thirty yards from the house along the old dry creek bed, was what appeared to be an old wooden lean-to. It probably had once been a farrowing house when someone raised pigs years before. The lean-to had been built fairly sturdy to begin with and had old wooden boards laid across the top and along the inside to reinforce the structure. This left a small opening in the front of the building at the top almost like a barn loft. I talked to Punkin as we cleaned on the little barn. I explained, "Sally will need a place to get away from anything or anyone who might want to hurt her. Sally will need to be warm at night while we sleep in the big house."

Suddenly, the realization of what I had said sank in, and Punkin asked, "Do you mean Sally's not going to sleep in our house anymore?"

Then I realized the good idea of building Sally a house outside was going to have some repercussions. I quickly passed the idea on to Punkin that Sally would be perfectly safe in her new house once we finished making it, and Sally had moved. Punkin kept working, but not with as much enthusiasm as when we first started. I could see thoughts of doubt going through Punkin's mind when I managed to get a glimpse of her face. One of the thoughts was, "Is building Sally a house outside really a good idea or not?"

When the small barn was cleaned out, we placed fresh prairie hay on the shelf we had built inside. We placed an old wooden door across the front so that the only access to the loft was the hole at the top of the small barn.

Sally was present during the whole process of working on the barn. She sniffed and scratched and played in every nook and cranny in the barn. Sally played in the new hay where we were making her bed. Occasionally during the project, Punkin would lose interest and wander off toward the dry creek bed behind the small barn. Sally would also lose her curiosity of new and different smells and would take off after Punkin at a slow lope, finally catching up to Punkin and nipping at her heels like a cow dog. Sally would jump in front of Punkin and roll in the sand as if she wanted Punkin to get on the ground to roll and play with her like Punkin would when Sally was in the big house. After a couple of these slow rolls, Punkin would bend over and pick Sally up. Sally would then lay her head on Punkin's shoulder and give a look of total contentment while she watched as the whole world passed them by.

Later that day I managed to find a log from a black locust tree that had fallen along the creek close to where the barn was located. I sawed a length of the log about eight feet long and leaned it into the hole at the top of the barn. The rest of the barn was totally sealed off, so Sally would need this locust post to get up to the entrance of her new home.

I called to Punkin, and she came running carrying Sally.

"Is Sally's house done, Daddy?" she asked.

"Yes, it is Punkin," I said. "Let's set Sally on the log and see if she will climb up and go inside."

Punkin placed Sally on the log facing the top of the post. Sally first flexed her muscles like a house cat and clawed at the bark on the locust pole like she was sharpening her claws. Sally gradually made her way to the top of the post. I noticed as Sally climbed up the pole that she was not as agile as I thought she would be. It was almost like watching Punkin when she tried her first lesson in how to ride a bicycle. Sally seemed unsure about climbing to that height on her own. She chattered a high pitched chatter of fear. Punkin had come to recognize this chatter of fear from Sally, so Punkin immediately went to rescue Sally from the locust log. I had to intervene and tell Punkin not to help her. Sally needed to learn to climb the log to her house by herself and all these lessons we were trying to teach Sally were for her own safety. Even though Punkin was only seven years old, I could see and recognize that motherly look on her face that said, "If that baby falls, it's going to be all your fault." Punkin and I finally convinced Sally to climb the locust pole. Sally made it up to her new house, wobbly legs and all.

Punkin and I could hear Sally rummaging around inside of her new home investigating all the contents. She had been on the inside of the barn for about five minutes when I suggested to Punkin we go inside and rest. We started walking toward the big house when Sally suddenly poked her head out from the small entrance to the barn loft of her new home. It was as if Sally knew she was being left behind. Punkin and I barely made it to our porch steps, and Sally was already on Punkin's heels nipping and playing. I was about to break the new rule and let Punkin bring Sally back into the house. All the while Punkin and Sally played, I was thinking, "Tonight, separating Punkin and Sally could be harder than I expected."

After supper our regular family routine was going on. I was lying on the couch reading, Mom was sewing and Punkin was in her room playing with Sally. Punkin carried Sally into the living room and sat down in the rocker with Sally on her lap. Later she placed Sally upon her shoulder and began go rock Sally to sleep. Sally would drape her body half way over Punkin's shoulder and flatten her body out along Punkin's neck as they rocked. Sally would go to sleep this way and sometimes snore loud enough to be heard across the room. The sound of the rocking chair and the rhythm of Sally's snores were broken by me speaking. I said, "Punkin, you do know Sally's going to sleep outside in her new home tonight, don't you?"

I was met with silence from Punkin.

I said, "Go put on your shoes and let's see if we can put her to bed in the new house."

Punkin and Sally met me at the back door. Holding the flashlight in my hand, I escorted Punkin and Sally on the long walk out to Sally's new home. I took Sally from Punkin's arms and placed her at the top of the locust post so she wouldn't have such a slow, wobbly climb to the top as she had before. Sally disappeared inside. I spoke to Punkin aloud and also to reassure myself.

"She'll be OK, Honey," I said. Then I grasped Punkin's hand and led her back into the house.

We had all been in bed less than thirty minutes when I heard that familiar scratch on the door. Sally would sometimes go out alone during the day but would usually spend less than ten minutes. Her signal to be let back in was a scratch on the door and a chatter of "I'm lost" or "I'm afraid." Along with the sound of Sally's chattering in the back ground, I heard small, soft footsteps approaching my side of the bed and then in the dark, a soft, frail voice.

"Daddy, Sally's crying on the porch. She's scratching and wants in," Punkin said.

"I know, Honey, but we can't let Sally in. She needs to learn to sleep in her own house," I said.

After a long, silent pause, I whispered, "Punkin go back to bed, Sally will be all right."

In a few more minutes, I could hear soft crying and tearful sniffles coming from Punkin's room. Sally's chattering and crying from outside had grown softer like she had physically worn herself out. I lay in bed and stared into the dark. I felt guilty, as if I had let both Punkin and Sally down. It was as though I had broken two hearts and planted a seed of distrust in both of them. It made me rethink the old philosophy of, "I'm doing this for your own good." Sometimes hearts don't understand that. Then I realized everything was quiet because both girls had cried themselves to sleep.

CHAPTER 9

The following couple of weeks proved to be a trying time for me. Sally and Punkin were an emotional pair. Punkin finally accepted that Sally could safely make it through the night without anything too drastic happening to her. Sally accepted her new found freedom of being a free roaming wild animal, and started enjoying the outdoors. Sometimes late in the night, I could hear Sally chattering in the distance or somewhere close around the house. She had always been extremely curious, but her stay outside made her become even more bold and adventurous. She played alone a lot now and seemed to venture farther away from home at night. Still, any loud noises or strange smells would send Sally racing to her sanctuary of the old barn loft. She was always present in her home by morning; overjoyed to see Punkin or me carrying out her favorite oatmeal and honey dish for breakfast. We very seldom had to call her name more than once to get a chattering response from inside her house. Usually she would simply react to the sound of the screen door opening and closing, plus the sound of footsteps on the old wooden porch. Sally would always emerge through the loft hole yawning and stretching. At the end of her awakening, she would give a small shiver.

It was amazing how much she had grown in less than two months. She had become a little overweight for a normal raccoon of her age. Sally had gotten so chunky that she was having trouble squeezing through the small barn loft hole. Each morning when Punkin and I went out to feed her, Sally forced her head and front shoulders through the hole and then would extend her long arms and paws forward as far as she could reach. Then Sally would give a chatter along with the look of "Don't just stand there; pull me out. I'm stuck." I would place my hands around her upper body like picking up a small child and pull her from the hole. When I pulled her out, she would immediately start rubbing her paws across my face in soft, smooth strokes as if she were saying, "Thank you."

Each morning I would pick Sally up and cuddle her close. While nuzzling in her fur, I would exclaim to Punkin, "Daddy always liked chunky girls," just to see if I could get a jealous reaction from Punkin. Punkin could see I was talking about Sally and would laugh and jump and try to pluck Sally from my arms. Then I would hold them both in my arms. I placed my head between both Sally's and Punkin's head and softly whispered, "You're my two best girls."

CHAPTER 10

Sally had gotten used to staying outside. Sometimes I would break my own rule though and let Sally come into the house when I was there by myself. This was one of those times I had violated the rules and let Sally in the house. I changed clothes and was preparing to go out into the garden and start working. Punkin and her mother were at grandma's house so Sally was alone with me. After the bathroom incident, Sally could not be trusted in the house alone anymore. I walked over to the couch where Sally was sleeping, reached down and picker her up.

She now weighed about 8 pounds. Her fur had become a more mature reddish brown and had black shiny tips. She had begun to get the full natural summer colors of a wild raccoon. The white patch of fur under her chin still set her apart from any other wild raccoon. The patch was almost a perfect triangle running from under her bottom jaw to the base of her throat. When Sally sat on her back legs in an upright position, she resembled a cinnamon colored brown bear and fro ma short distance, the white triangle patch beneath her chin seemed to make it even more so. I carried Sally out of the big house to the garden with me and set her down. It had gotten to a point that someone needed to watch her constantly. I turned the water on the rows of corn and squash while Sally played.

While I was working in the garden, Sally hadn't made any "lost calls" in the last few minutes, so I hadn't really paid any particular attention to her whereabouts. I finished hoeing out to the end of a corn row when Sally caught my attention. Sally was crossing the main yard in front of the big house. Her nose was about an inch off the ground and pressing hard to catch up to what rural people in this area had always called cow ants.

These so-called cow ants were about one inch long and covered with long red furry hair. The rest of their body was black furry hair. Cow ants are very attractive insects, but as in most cases in the animal and insect world, anything attractive is usually deadly. Cow ants can deliver a brutally painful sting. I immediately started to cross the yard and catch up to Sally. As if I were talking to a little kid, I yelled at Sally, "You had better leave that thing alone. It'll sting you!"

I managed to catch up to Sally before she caught up to the cow ant. I pushed Sally with my foot to try and discourage her interest in the cow ant. Sally balled up around my foot like she always did with Punkin's, as if I had made this trip across the yard to play. I shook Sally off my foot, and she chattered, but foot wrestling was not what was on her mind. She immediately went back to the cow ant. This time I picked up Sally when I finally managed to catch her. My verbal threats were not an intimidation. I carried Sally back to the ends of the corn rows and set her down. Even the trickling water couldn't hold her attention. Like a flash she was back across the yard to the cow ant. I thought to myself, "Punkin's not here to save you, so you probably need to learn this for yourself, little girl."

That thought had no more than cleared my mind when I heard a loud squalling sound come from the other end of the yard. I walked to the edge of the corn rows to catch the action. Sally had managed to get the cow ant, stinger and all, firmly implanted on the soft portion of skin just above her nose. I could tell from the dust flying and all the squeals and squalls that Sally was getting a real lesson. After about twenty seconds of rolling, swatting and squalling, Sally made a mad dash for the front porch. I don't know if Sally got away from the ant or if the ant got away from Sally, but it was a mutual parting. Sally was standing on her hind feet reaching up as high as she could on the screen door and scratching with both paws. This was Sally's signal to Punkin that she wanted in the house. Punkin wasn't home. I called to Sally a couple of time and finally managed to get her attention. She didn't want me; she wanted her Mamma, "Punkin."

I managed to catch Sally and take her into the house and get her nose doctored. The ant bite had already begun to swell. My medical chores were finished none too soon. The pickup truck coming into the driveway was carrying Punkin and her mother. I stepped out on the front porch carrying Sally and started back toward the garden. I was met by Punkin who plucked Sally from my arms. We all three went back to the corn and squash rows in the garden. The girls began making mud pies, and I began hoeing. While hoeing close to where the girls were sitting, I unearthed an even larger cow ant. It started running toward the place where both girls were sitting and playing. Upon spying the large red critter, both gals gave a squeal and the ant right-of-way as he raced by. Sally seemed to give up an even wider area than Punkin did.

As we all watched the large cow ant crawl away, Punkin exclaimed, "Daddy, isn't Sally smart? Look! She knows those cow ants can bite."

I never said a word. I just kept on hoeing.

CHAPTER 11

It was the middle of summer now, and Sally was about three-fourths grown. She was still a lot bitter, weight wise than any normal wild raccoon her age. It had become a burden for Punkin to carry her around, but Sally still expected special treatment. The summer rains had filled some of the red clay potholes in the normally dry creek bed behind our house. Punkin learned that one of Sally's favorite things to do was to travel from pothole to pothole along the creek bed and investigate the new territory. I gave them a little more freedom than normal because the creek bed was less than thirty yards form our house and the water in the potholes was less than three inches deep at any given point. Even with all this new freedom, Punkin nor Sally ever got out of my eyesight.

Occasionally I would accompany Punkin and Sally to the creek bed. On our trips, I always pointed out to Punkin some of the things nature had provided for Sally because I knew there would come a time that Sally would need to find her own food and not depend on Punkin or me to provide the oatmeal dish.

On one of our trips to the creek, Punkin and I were following Sally from pothole to pothole watching her smell down into every clay hole she came to. Sally's natural instincts of being a wild raccoon always took over when Punkin and I accompanied her. Sally would bristle with excitement. She needed to explore anything that seemed out of place to her. I am sure part of the excitement was the smell of other animals that had come to the potholes to drink or look for food during the night. Occasionally, we would see small footprints and evidence of where other raccoons had come to the potholes.

The summer rains had filled the clay crawfish holes located higher up on the creek banks. During the rains, the crawfish left these holes and went to the potholes of water in the creek. Punkin watched Sally for hours over the summer while Sally went from crawfish hole to crawfish hole. Sally would first smell the hole where the crawfish placed its small round goblets of mud around the top. Then she ran her small slender arm as far into the hole as she could reach. These small crawfish holes were only large enough to get one slender arm and paw into at one time. Sally would not pass a crawfish hole without a full length search into the small water filled cavity with her paw. While moving from crawfish hole to crawfish hole, she would occasionally get distracted from her fishing by a grasshopper that had fallen into the creek bed. When Sally found one of these grasshoppers, she would immediately carry her prey to one of the potholes of water to wash it off before she ate it. I had always heard from some the older woodsmen in my life that a raccoon would always try to wash its food before eating it. Sally seemed to have proven this theory because no matter what she found along the creek bed, she took it to one of the potholes and washed it off before trying to eat it. At the end of these trips, Sally was always covered with red clay mud. It would be matted into her fur on both arms and around her nose and face where she would bury her nose and face into the crawfish holes to get a better smell. At the end of each trip and after her bath, I remembered why Sally had her own house.

On one of these trips to the creek, Punkin and I were slowly walking behind Sally. Sally was making her way along the creek bed about ten feet in front of us, searching out every pothole and every crawfish hole that she came to. Sally had made her way farther up the creek bed than we had ever gone before. Sally found a place where fresh water dribbled out of an old irrigation canal into the creek bed. There were numerous small flat rocks that surrounded a larger pothole that was about five feet across. Sally was playing and sniffing along the edge of the water and around the flat rocks. All of a sudden she seemed to pay particular attention to a larger flat rock about twelve inches across in two directions. The rock was thin and didn't look very heavy. Sally had lain down along the side of the rock and extended her left arm as far under the rock as she could reach. We could see a look of excitement on her face. She pulled her arm from under the rock and went all along the edges digging and probing trying to find a way to get under the rock.

After a couple of minutes we could see and feel how desperate Sally was becoming to get under the rock. She looked over at Punkin and gave a high-pitched chatter asking for help. Punkin started to get up from where she was sitting and at the same time said, "Daddy, I think there's something under that rock Sally wants."

I said, "Yes, there probably is, but first let Sally see if she can get it out by herself."

Sally became more frustrated and chattered more than usual at Punkin, but I wouldn't let Punkin interfere.

Finally, in desperation, Sally placed both paws under the edge of the rock and lifted it with her whole chunky body. The rock flipped over and there underneath were the results of all Sally's summer labor, a large red male crawfish about five inches long. The crawfish had his pinchers extended and lifted into the air. Both claws were open and ready for combat. He was trying to slowly back toward the pothole of water without drawing too much attention to himself.

Sally's eyes were glued to the crawfish's movement. This was to be her reward for all the hours of searching potholes and water filled holes. Sally slowly lowered her head to get a sniff of her newly uncovered treasure. That was her first mistake in crawdad fishing. The large crawfish pinched down with both pinchers. One pincher was tightly locked on her lip and the other one tightly clamped on her nose. Sally squalled and slung her head back, then rapidly from side to side, trying to get the crawfish to release his grip from her face. After two or three quick tries, she succeeded.

All of the time this lesson for Sally was going on, I had my arms wrapped around Punkin to keep her from going to Sally's rescue. I could feel Punkin's muscles tighten under my wrapped arms, and I would softly say, "Punkin, Sally needs to know this. She'll be OK."

After slinging the crawfish from her face, Sally looked at Punkin and me with a look on her face that said, "You didn't tell me these things would bite!"

After being from ejected from Sally's face, the crawfish landed about four feet away from the pothole of water. Upon the crawfish's landing, he decided to make a little hastier retreat back to the pothole of water because his luck was running out.

While the crawfish was making his move backwards toward the hole of water, his pinchers were still held at a combat ready position. Sally was still staring at the crawfish's movement and trying to decide what to do about it. She looked over at Punkin and me and gave an "I need help" chatter. All the while the crawfish was getting closer to the water. Sally stared at the crawfish intently with a look of, "You're not gonna get away with that!" Then she suddenly leaped, pushing off with her hind feet and landed full force on top of the crawfish. Sally made a made a couple of desperate swipes with each paw as if to knock the crawfish back away from the water.

The crawfish was flipping his whole body into the air using his tail to propel himself off the ground. Sally was slapping and pawing at the crawfish as he flipped his way back toward the pool. In one lucky instant, the crawfish flipped in the right direction and …kerplunk… he landed back into the water.

Sally stared quietly at the circular ripples on top of the pool. Then she stared at Punkin and me with the look of a fisherman's tale that said, "The big one has just gotten away."

We could feel Sally's disappointment of her first real crawfish getting away. Sally just stopped and looked with amazement at the ripple on top of the water where her prize had disappeared. Then slowly and without a lot of enthusiasm, Sally strolled off into the small pool. She began her ritual of extending her arms and feeling in every direction as she crossed the pool. On her first pass she stopped at the center of the pool and made a motion under the water with her hands like she was rolling marbles on the floor at home. Sally, half submerged in the water, turned and faced Punkin and me. She seemed to have a special gleam in her eye and a large grin on her face. It was that fisherman's look again. This time the look said, "You're not gonna believe this, but this pothole of water is full of crawfish."

Sally, Punkin and I spent the rest of the afternoon at the pool. Sally would chase the crawfish close to shore and then slap them out onto dry land. Along with the help of Punkin, not too many crawfish escaped back into the pool. Once on the ground Punkin would assist while Sally pounced on each crawfish crushing them and then eating their soft meaty tails. The next few hours were spent by Sally and Punkin chasing crawdads around in the water filled clay pothole.

It was beginning to get dark. The evening shadows were becoming long, extending all the way across the creek bed. Both the girls were covered in red clay mud, yet neither girl wanted to leave when I reminded them it was getting late and we needed to start back toward home.

"Just let us catch one more, Daddy!" Punkin exclaimed.

After I let them catch one more crawfish, I still had to physically retrieve Sally from the pool and carry her away, eventually making it back to the house. By the time we arrived, I was carrying Punkin on my back and Sally in my arms. I set them both down in the yard and sprayed them both clean with the garden hose. Mom brought out a couple of towels. Punkin toweled off and went into the house with Mom. I carried Sally to her house and dried her off with the towel. After being hand dried, Sally's fur would always feel so soft and fluffy. Then I set her up on the pole, and she disappeared inside the loft. Punkin was already asleep on the couch when I went into the house. Lying there in a deep sleep, Punkin's snores were as soft and rhythmic as Sally's. I reached down and gave Punkin a kiss and softly whispered, "Fishing sure is hard work for Daddy's girls."

CHAPTER 12

It was later summer now. Sally and Punkin had become quite efficient fishermen. Punkin would usually share some of their more exciting adventures at the end of each fishing trip. Occasionally fishing tales of a garter snake or a leopard frog would be told. Punkin and Sally had also had to expand their friendship to a threesome.

My Dad had adopted a small, red baby pig from of my nephews. This small pig was the runt of a litter of eight piglets. Arnold, the pig, was used to being fed with a baby milk bottle like Sally's. The task of baby sitting Arnold for a couple of weeks while my folks were away was appointed to Punkin and me because we had "so much experience at bottle feeding animals."

Arnold's temporary visit turned out to be more of a war than a friendly family visit the first couple of days. Sally wasn't sure about other animals-especially Arnold. To my knowledge the only other animals Sally had seen were a few cows that were in the field located across the black-top road from the big house. Sally had managed to run into a skunk or two at night while outside alone, but, other than those few contacts, Sally knew nothing at all about other animals.

The first day Arnold came to the big house, Sally was a little fearful but also quite curious. Arnold had arrived early in the morning. It seemed as if Arnold's whole existence evolved around eating and sleeping. This was not true with Sally. Sally was a thinker and a doer. Sally's entire first day with Arnold was spent by lying on top of her barn stretched out sunning on her locust pole, watching and analyzing his unfamiliar activities. Arnold spent most of his first day rooting around in the yard or sleeping.

It was late evening and time for Sally and Arnold both to be fed. I carried Sally's oatmeal dish out and set it on top of her small barn. She chattered happily as I arrived with dinner. Sally was halfway through with her supper when Punkin came out on the porch carrying a large baby milk bottle. The movement of Punkin squatting on the bottom steps of the porch and letting Arnold attack a large bottle of milk caught Sally's attention immediately. Sally didn't know a lot about pigs, but she did know about Punkin and large bottles of milk. Sally had a bird's eye view of Punkin, Arnold and the milk bottle from where she sat atop her barn. I don't know if it was jealousy or hunger that drove Sally from her perch. From my vantage point, all I could see was a look on Sally's face that said, "That's my Momma and my milk bottle, and that pig is trying to steal them both." We had taught Sally a lot of things but how to share was not one of them.

Quick as a flash, Sally was off the top of the barn, down the post and sitting astride Arnold's back. The pig was so engulfed in gulping down supper he never paid any attention to Sally sitting in the middle of his back. It was a "Kodak moment"!

Sally lay flat out against Arnold's back and placed a tiny paw over each one of the pig's eyes. Then Sally started a long hard pull to try and break the suction that Arnold had on the baby milk bottle. The harder Sally tried to pull Arnold back away from the bottle, the faster Arnold gulped. Finally, suction broke. At the first slight opening between Arnold and the milk bottle, Sally made her play. She lunged forward toward the bottle while shoving Arnold backward. Sally immediately attached her mouth to the large rubber nipple and clenched down tight with her teeth. Both of her paws were firmly holding to the black lid ring of the milk bottle. A counter attack was soon launched by Arnold. The charge from Arnold's short stout body into Sally's side knocked Sally loose from the bottle, but the charge also jarred the milk bottle loose from Punkin's hands. The milk bottle rolled to the bottom steps of the porch and stopped. A few seconds later Sally and Arnold both went for the milk bottle at the same time.

What followed was our first grunting, squealing, squalling raccoon-pig fight. While I held the dynamic duo apart, Punkin ran quickly into the house and got another bottle of milk. From that point on, as long as we had two bottles of milk and fed Sally and Arnold at the same time on separate ends of the porch steps, the milk bottle wars subsided. For the next two weeks, we only saw an occasional temper flare up from the two. That is, as long as both Sally's and Arnold's bellies were full and Arnold didn't try to "hog" too much of Punkin's attention, Arnold and Sally remained pretty good friends.

During the two weeks of Arnold's stay, I would be outside hoeing in the garden and each evening I would see Punkin, Sally and Arnold coming from out of the old rain soaked creek bed after a hard day of fishing. I watched the mud covered trio climb the dirt bank behind the big house to the end of the garden where I was working. As I watched the trio emerge from the rain soaked creek bed and to the end of the garden, I would think to myself, "This is just like having my own personal Ellie Mae Clampett."

CHAPTER 13

Summer was almost over. Arnold had been gone almost a month now, and things around the big house had finally gotten back to normal. Everyone enjoyed Arnold's stay, but we were all happy to see him go.

Punkin and Sally were still an inseparable pair and spent most of their time together every day. Sally kept growing and getting bigger, now weighing about fifteen pounds. She changed her diet from oatmeal and honey to about anything Punkin or I took out to her barn. She became especially fond of dog food since it was mostly ground corn anyway. Sally had gotten so she wanted her meals delivered to the top of her barn as opposed to just setting the food on the ground in her bowl. It also became apparent by the amount of food we delivered to the barn that Sally had friends coming over.

Sometimes in the night while lying in bed with the window open, I heard other raccoons chattering among the corn rows out in the garden. I also saw evidence of where other raccoons left tiny tracks in the garden in the fresh mud between the rows. Sally had became a very late sleeper. Usually upon the sound of Punkin or myself leaving the big house with her food, Sally would meet us at the top of the locust pole for breakfast or lunch. But lately Sally ignored our dinner calls and would sleep in until about noon or later. Sally was spending some of her nights away from home with her raccoon friends. Even though I knew there were dangers involved when Sally was away from home, I wanted Sally to be free, and I was not about to confine her to a cage or try and tie her up. I wanted Sally to become as free and wild as possible and still remain close friends with Punkin. I felt assured that Sally was learning some life saving skills from the other wild raccoons she had been associating with. With as much time as Sally was spending away from home, I knew that she was really getting to know the wild side of life.

School was going to start back in a few days. That meant Sally would be home by herself a lot again. Punkin would be in school, and her mother and I would be away from home working most of the day. I had given some thought to Sally's safety while everyone was away from home, but I knew Sally would be completely safe as long as she stayed close to her barn loft.

Earlier that summer, I had promised to take Punkin and Sally to the Canadian River swimming before school started back in the fall. Today looked like the perfect day. There was plenty of sunshine, very little wind, and it was hot. So an afternoon swim seemed like a fun trip for all of us. I caught Sally and handed her to Punkin, who was sitting in the front seat of my truck. Sally was nervous because this was her first actual ride in a vehicle since I had brought her home.

The only times Sally had actually been swatted when she had gotten around the vehicles parked in the yard at the big house. I wanted Sally to remain afraid of vehicles because cars and trucks were so dangerous for her to be around. After some comforting from Punkin during the ride, we arrived at the river with Sally's nerves calmed. I took Sally and Punkin to a place on the river that was safe for their swimming lessons. The water at this particular stretch of the river was only about three feet deep. The water here was crystal clear with a solid sand bottom and long, flat sandy beaches along each side of the pool, almost like the ocean. The pool of water where we decided to try our swimming lesson was about 50 yards long. At the upper end of the pool was a large log jam of driftwood lodged in the center of the river. It had been placed there by all the spring floods earlier in the year.

Punkin and I waded off into the edge of the river with hands locked firmly together, while Sally played along the sandy river shore. The water here, close to the river's edge, was only about two feet deep. Punkin and I were lying in the water on our backs while we watched Sally run the sandy river banks. With so many new and different smells, Sally couldn't make up her mind which set of new smells she wanted to pursue. I had never seen Sally so excited. All the new smells of the river turned her into a total fur ball of energy. After a short time of chasing her imaginary friends up and down the river bank, Sally decided to come out and join Punkin and me for a swim.

Sally left the shallower water and started out to where Punkin was laughing and splashing in the deeper water. About a foot from the water's edge, Sally realized her feet were no longer touching bottom. For the first time since Sally had been with us, I actually saw fear on her face. Sally immediately started to chatter as she swam toward Punkin. The natural flow of the river's current was pulling Sally down the river and away from us all the time she was trying to swim out to Punkin. The area below us that Sally was floating toward was less than three inches deep. Sally was chattering at Punkin to come and save her, but I wouldn't let Punkin go to Sally's rescue just yet. I knew eventually Sally's feet would touch bottom again, and she would be fine. Finally, Sally's feet touched bottom on the sand shoal she had drifted down to. She waded from the shoal back to shore, stopped and stared back up river at Punkin and me. Sally had a look on her face that said, "I can't believe you almost let me drown. I don't think I like this deep water."

Sally quickly ran the river's edge back to where Punkin and I were playing in the water. She still wanted to come out to where Punkin was swimming and splashing around in the river. This time, after Sally decided to try and swim out to Punkin, she moved about thirty yards farther up the river bank. Once there, Sally hesitated a bit then waded into the deeper water. As Sally swam by Punkin this time, she had a much happier look on her face. Sally's tiny feet were paddling away below her chunky body in the clear water, and on her face was a big smile of pride that said, "Look at me; I can swim!"

Sally spent the next 30 minutes making large race track maneuvers. She ran the river's edge back to about 40 yards above where Punkin and I were swimming before she would enter the water again. Then Sally would plunge off into the deep, as if she was no longer afraid of the water. After each pass of swimming past Punkin and me and landing on the shore below, Sally would quickly run the river's edge to complete another circle. As Sally swam by, Punkin would scream and splash water at Sally. Punkin would yell, "Look Daddy, Sally loves to swim just like me."

To me personally, this day was building a memory that would last a lifetime – a swim at the beach with my two best girls.

CHAPTER 14

The three of us, Sally, Punkin and I, were able to make three more trips to the river before Punkin's return to school. Sally and Punkin both loved the water and became quite proficient at swimming. Since Sally, Punkin and I were all the adventurous type, we took long walks along the river during our evening swimming trips. While on these trips, Sally investigated everything along the river's edge. Punkin and I simply walked the sandy shores looking for snail shells or Indian artifacts such as pottery chips, flint chips, or old bone fragments.

On one of these side trips, Punkin and I walked the river's shallow sand beaches while Sally ran the opposite shore. Sally left no stick or stone unturned or passed any crawfish hole without first feeling into the hole with her tiny paws. Sometimes, she totally disappeared into a hollow dirt hole under the root covered river banks where the entrance to an old beaver den had been exposed. On our last trip to the river, Punkin and I stopped at a spot along a clay shoal at the river's edge where an unusually large amount of flint chips and bone fragments were exposed on top of the sand. Punkin was busy collecting pretty rocks, which usually ended up in my pockets to save, while I browsed through the flint chips to look for arrowheads or scrapers made by the American Indians, the earlier inhabitants along the Canadian River. Sally stopped on the opposite shore and was playing and digging along a steep clay bluff.

Sally kept smelling and digging with both paws trying to dislodge something from the blue clay mud. I thought Sally was just being her persistent self by trying to dig out a large crawfish imbedded in the clay. After five minutes of watching Sally dig, I said to Punkin, "Sally must have a large crawfish located in the hole where she keeps digging." I watched a while longer and decided I should wade across the river and help her. On my way over to Sally, I picked up a small stick floating along the river's edge that had drifted down from a beaver lodge located farther up the river. I picked up the stick thinking I could use it to assist Sally in digging up the crawfish she found. I climbed the slick clay bank to where Sally was still digging. When I was close enough, I noticed a small hole going down into the heavy clay mud where Sally had constantly been digging and pawing the last few minutes. As I knelt I could see in the shale mud what appeared to be the edge of a small white rock. Sally had managed to clean a small area out away from the rock and was still digging. My presence didn't seem to distract Sally away from her task at all. She seemed extremely focused on this object. I immediately started to help Sally dig. Splashing water along the hole's edges where Sally was digging, I used my stick as a pry bar to break up the clay around the object's edges.

The excitement of Sally and me digging made Punkin wade across the river to where we both were now slinging lots of mud.

"What did Sally find, Daddy?" Punkin asked.

"I don't know exactly," I told Punkin. "It looks like some kind of animal skull. It could be a cow skull or maybe a large bull's skull," I said.

I had already been able to partially uncover the front part of what appeared to be a skull of some kind. Sally, Punkin and I kept digging along side each other, and the skull kept getting larger. We had so far uncovered part of the face, an eye socket and one large horn. After cleaning off the horn, I took a closer look at the full skull that had been uncovered, It was then I realized what a real treasure Sally had found.

"It's a huge buffalo head!" I exclaimed.

In another full hour of careful excavation, we could all see the efforts of our work lying in front of us, because there lying at our feet was a full buffalo skull. The skull had all of its teeth firmly in place. The skull was partially petrified from the thousands of years of being buried in the oil shale clay along the river. What was amazing was that the skull was totally intact!

I looked at Punkin and said, "Since the day we found Sally, she has brought us nothing but joy and good luck!"

Then I reached down and quickly fluffed the hair behind Sally's neck and on top of her head, just like aunts and uncles used to do to us all when we were kids. Sally, just like all of us, hated it. Sally chattered and balled up around my hand like she was attacking. Punkin bent down and picked up Sally, and I picked up the buffalo head. Punkin and I both congratulated Sally on her excellent find as we all started back down the river to the truck.

CHAPTER 15

Sally never actually got over Punkin abandoning her for school. What Sally didn't know was that school was not exactly Punkin's choice either. The first few weeks were traumatic on Sally. She would chatter while going all the way around the house, scratching on all the doors, and fully expecting Punkin to come charging out of the house to play. Sally's old approach of scratching and chattering, no matter how high pitched it became, could not bring Punkin from the house. Gradually, Sally and Punkin were spending less time together. With all Sally's free time, she went back to her other friends for companionship. Sally actually began to stay away from home for two or three nights at a time. In the morning when Punkin rushed off to catch the bus, I would go out to Sally's barn to retrieve her oatmeal bowl only to find hard dried oatmeal in her dish. My mind would wander off to try and guess where Sally was, and what she was doing.

From the first day I found Sally, it had always been my full intention to set her totally free one day without any attachments. Sally had been with us so long now though, I knew it would be hard for Punkin and me to set her free. Punkin and I both had grown very attached to Sally. I guess I hated to admit it, but I loved Sally too.

Sally returned home after spending a few nights away, and we could hear her out by her barn chattering. If her chattering was ignored, Sally sometimes came and scratched on the door. Punkin always squealed with delight when she heard Sally's chattering, and ran through the house to the front porch and would yell, "Daddy, Sally's back, Sally's home."

Standing on the wooden porch, I watched as the two tried to make up for the separation. Punkin would love, squeeze and hug on Sally while Sally rolled over onto her back in Punkin's arms. Sally would chatter and make the small rubbing motions with her paws along Punkin's cheeks as she always had done. Then while Punkin held her, Sally would softly nip at Punkin's chin with small, playful bites. It was as if their making up for ignoring each other was almost as good as all the quality time the two spent together previously. I guess I had grown soft and sympathetic to their cause of separation, because on occasion I would break the rule again and let Punkin bring Sally into the house and rock her to sleep in the big chair like Sally was still Punkin's baby. Even with the separation of school and friends, Sally and Punkin were still an inseparable pair.

CHPATER 16

Sally's visits home to her barn became less and less frequent. Occasionally I found Sally's empty oatmeal bowl overturned on top of her barn. There would also be evidence around her barn where Sally brought friends over for dinner. Punkin and I still kept Sally's larger bowl of dog food on top of her barn where no other animals could get access to her food. On weekends, Punkin always checked to see if Sally had been home during the week without Punkin knowing it. Sometimes during the week, I would see Punkin walking around Sally's barn and looking into the loft to see if Sally was home. On occasion I heard Punkin calling Sally's name into the loft trying to raise a chatter from inside. This was just in case Sally happened to be inside her loft and was simply sleeping in. No chatters were ever heard from inside the loft so Punkin would simply hang her head in disappointment and slowly walk away.

Reclining in the big chair one night reading, I thought I heard a faint chattering of a raccoon somewhere outside in the dark. Sally had not been home to sleep overnight in her barn for quite some time. Until I was sure of what I was hearing, I didn't notify Punkin. I did not want to sound a false alarm and build up Punkin's hopes of the possibility of Sally's being home. I walked slowly to the bay windows and looked out into the yard along the edge of the shadows created by our yard's vapor light. It was then I noticed Sally and one of her friends sneaking along the shadows edge heading toward Sally's barn and her food bowl.

Quickly stepping to the hallway of the house, I yelled at Punkin. "Come here, quick. Hurry!"

A few seconds later Punkin appeared in the doorway. Punkin had a look of expectation on her face but really didn't know yet what to expect as I led her to the big windows in the front room. Sally and her friend had already reached the middle of our yard and were in plain view of Punkin and me. Sally's friend was in the lead and Sally was attacking his heels from behind, just as she had always done with Punkin on their walks together. When Sally caught up to the other raccoon, they would both tumble and roll together on the yellow dead grass.

"Is that one of Sally's friends, Daddy?" Punkin asked.

"Yes, Honey," I answered. "That's probably Sally's boyfriend. The one Sally's been spending all her time with lately," I said.

As the two raccoons rolled and chattered and growled and fussed, Punkin and I watched from the bay window. I could tell by the big grin on Punkin's face that she had given her approval of Sally's choice of boyfriends.

"Can I go out and play with them?" Punkin asked.

"If you go outside, you'll probably scare Sally's friend away," I said.

I could tell by how fidgety Punkin was getting that my answer wasn't good enough to satisfy her. I finally made myself give in to Punkin's pressure. "Go ahead," I said, "but go slowly."

Punkin quietly eased out the front door onto the wooden porch. The sight of Punkin standing in the shadows broke up Sally's wrestling match with her friend. As I watched closely, the two raccoons parted company. One raccoon quickly rushed toward the dark and the other started slowly toward Punkin. Sally had evidently become a little more wild because Punkin had to coax Sally to come close enough for Punkin to touch her. Once Sally felt Punkin's little hands touch her soft fur, it was back to being old friends. Sally's boyfriend stopped at the edge of the darkness and watched with amazement at what Sally was doing. He could not believe his eyes or that his chattering pleas were being ignored by Sally. While Punkin and Sally loved on each other, Sally's friend nervously paced the edge of darkness. Sally eventually became restless in Punkin's arms and gave in to her friends whines and chatters. Punkin took a few steps forward, then gave Sally a long hard squeeze and released Sally onto the ground.

Sally scampered toward her friend who was waiting in the dark. She loped only a few yards before stopping, looked back toward Punkin and made a pleading, whining sound. Sally then retreated back toward Punkin for a few steps and started chattering loudly. Sally whirled away from Punkin to head into the darkness to her friend, but with each whirling turn Sally looked back and chattered like she wanted Punkin to follow. It was as if each girl were being drawn toward separate worlds. Punkin followed Sally halfway across the yard and stopped. Sally looked back and chattered one final plea at Punkin and disappeared off into the darkness with her friend. Punkin stood alone as if hypnotized, staring into the dark night. I noticed Punkin's small hands raise to her face to wipe away the tears as she turned back toward the big house. It was if at that moment Punkin knew in her heart Sally had made a very tough choice, and the choice Sally had made was to be free.

CHAPTER 17

It was Christmas Eve. Punkin had gone to bed, almost an hour before, with all sorts of images of what would be under the tree for her on Christmas morning. The excitement and anticipation had worn Punkin out, so I had tucked her into bed. Earlier that afternoon, it had snowed about three inches. I was standing and looking outside through the bay windows at the moon's glow beaming down on the yard. The glow gave a beautiful blue tint to everything. I had just finished my dutiful chores as Santa, placing packages both big and small beneath the Christmas tree. Staring across the snow covered yard, I looked forward to the excitement of tomorrow morning and how excited I knew Punkin would be.

Then I heard that old familiar sound of a muffled chatter coming from out on the wooden porch. Walking to the front door, I saw lots of tiny hand prints made by a raccoon in the snow on the porch steps. By the tracks left in the snow, the raccoon had made a couple of wandering circles on our porch, traveled down the steps to the bottom and turned north toward Sally's barn. Were these tracks made by Sally or some other raccoon? Neither Punkin nor I had actually seen Sally for about two months. Even when Sally returned home she was so wild no one could catch her or pick her up except Punkin. Punkin's mother and I could get close to her, but Sally always stayed just out of reach.

Walking into the kitchen I set a pan of milk on the stove to warm. If this raccoon was Sally, she would be hungry and probably stay close to home until Punkin or I fed her. Leaving the big house, I walked out to Sally's house with a mush made of oatmeal, honey, and warm milk. Following the small set of footprints, I walked out to the locust pole leading up to Sally's loft. There were no other tracks. I assumed these tracks were Sally's, and she had come home for food and a safe place for a long winter nap. I moved in close to the opening that led to Sally's loft.

"Sally, is that you in there? Come out here, Honey." I said.

My voice was met with a weak chatter. I placed the oatmeal bowl near the entrance to Sally's loft so the steam and the smell from the mush could enter her house. A short time later at the entrance, Sally's head popped out. That small white tuft of hair under her chin was visible even in the dim light. Sally's fur looked so pretty and smooth just like always. Her winter coat was long, dark, and warm. Backing away from the barn, I set the bowl of mush on the ground near the end of the locust pole. Sally immediately descended from her lofty perch to the bowl below. While I stood about five feet away, Sally licked away at the oatmeal mush. Sally ate like she was starving, but from looking at her size and sleek winter coat, her actually starving was the farthest thing from the truth.

When Sally finished her warm meal, she returned to the bottom of the locust pole, started up and stopped. Then she made an acrobatic move, turned around on the log and headed back down the pole and out to where I was standing. Kneeling down, I extended my hand to see if she would let me touch her. She hesitated a moment at first, and then she walked closer to me like letting me touch her was a "thank you" for bringing her a hot meal.

Reaching over, I picked up Sally for the first time in about four months. Pulling her close and hugging her, I buried my face into the fur at the base of her neck as I did when she was small. Sally's natural odor was fresh, sweet, and clean. This moment of holding her made me feel like I had gotten to hug a long lost friend and didn't really want to be the first to stop hugging. While I was hugging Sally, she placed her feet alongside my neck, and at first touch they felt as if they were frozen. Even though her paws were wet and extremely cold, they felt soft and comfortable against my neck. I could feel the layer of body fat Sally stored for winter beneath her thick fur coat. While I was feeling of Sally's body fat, my hands ran across something else. Sally's milk glands that ran along the underside of her body were becoming long, hard ridges. Several small hard knots could also be felt at the base of Sally's stomach. When I finally realized what I was feeling, my heart jumped with joy. Sally was going to be a mother!

I set Sally at the upper end of the locust pole, gave her a pat on the back and said, "You're my girl, Honey."

Sally gave a quiet chatter and disappeared inside her loft. The following morning when Punkin jumped from her bed, the first news she got was that Sally came home during the night and was out in her barn loft. Standing before me was an eight year old girl who had a huge decision to make. Punkin's mind raced; should she run to see Sally, or open all her Christmas presents. It seemed like a toss up until I mentioned I thought Sally was going to have babies. Evidently from Punkin's actions, she must have thought I meant Sally was in the act of having her babies right then because out the front door and down the front steps she flew, headed for Sally's house. Christmas presents were no competition for Sally and her babies. After a closer examination of Sally by Punkin, the whole rest of the day was consumed by questions, the most prominent question being, "Daddy, when's Sally gonna have her babies?"

CHAPTER 18

Sally remained close to home all the time Punkin was on Christmas vacation from school. Punkin and Sally spent a great deal of time outside together playing. Neither girl really liked the cold weather though, so Punkin spent most of her time inside the big house and Sally stayed in her barn and slept a lot. Sally sometimes slept two or three days at a time without actually emerging from her house to eat or play with Punkin. Usually Punkin could not stand to stay out in the cold long enough to persuade Sally to come out and play. It seemed Sally would much rather sleep than come out into the cold for few precious minutes and play with Punkin. Winter was quite a contrast from their usual summer time activities.

A day of above average temperature came along occasionally and the girls spent the entire day outside. On these bluebird days, Punkin and Sally took their short hikes in back of the big house along the dry creek bed, as they had during the past summer. It was these special days that I could tell Punkin and Sally forgot about school and friends and the separation these other interests had caused them. Time seemed to be standing still for both Punkin and Sally, and they were taking advantage of it.

After a few weeks of rest and recuperation, Sally again began to roam. She stayed away from home for two weeks or longer without coming home for food or shelter. I began to wonder if Sally had picked a hollow tree or snag somewhere along a creek bottom to have her kittens. I always felt when it was time for Sally to have her kitten, she would return to a place where she knew her kittens would be safe and welcome, and that place would be home with Punkin and me.

It had been almost a full month since I had seen any activity around Sally's barn that would lead me to believe either Sally or any of her friends had come around to sleep or eat the dog food Punkin and I left out for her. In the late evenings, I would sometimes catch a glimpse of Punkin standing in front of the window in her room, staring out toward Sally's house. She stood for extended periods of time without moving or saying a word; just staring out toward Sally's barn. Her small hands would be tightly wrapped around the wooden seal in the middle of the window. When the window fogged over, it would usually break Punkin's concentration. It was like she was scanning her thoughts of where Sally could be and what Sally could be doing. Some of these thoughts also crossed my mind, plus one I didn't want to share with Punkin. Sally may have turned totally wild and would never again return home? I anticipated Punkin someday asking about Sally, but she never did. When Sally's name popped up in a conversation, it was always met with a positive response from Punkin. She would just calmly look at me and say, "Daddy, Sally will come back home because she loves me." It was then I knew a child's faith in love was stronger than that of most adults.

CHAPTER 19

It was now late spring. The huge cotton wood and oak trees along the creek had full leaves. In the evenings, we could hear the rustling of the cotton wood leaves from the wooden porch when the wind would softly blow through them. The smell of spring was in the air. Sally returned home only once after her Christmas visit with Punkin. From that point on, I had my doubts that Sally would ever return, but Punkin still held her positive outlook. She religiously checked Sally's dog food bowl to see if Sally had made any late night visits. The dog food was sometimes gone, and Punkin would be convinced Sally had made a visit home. Not wanting to destroy Punkin's fantasy, I didn't tell her I saw a large opossum visiting Sally's food bowl on a regular basis at night when Punkin was sound asleep. So I let Punkin believe Sally was sneaking around the barn late in the night and was just being unsociable because of her snooty friends. Walking by Sally's barn one day, I noticed the food bowl had been turned upside down on top of her barn. Turning the bowl over was something opossums didn't usually do. Always when Sally finished her meal, she would turn the bowl over, as if to look underneath to see if there might be anything under the bowl to eat. Obviously she learned this trick from getting crawfish out from under rocks along the creek. Moving closer to Sally's barn, I called inside the loft, "Sally, did you come home, Honey?"

To my surprise, a chatter come from inside the barn. Sally couldn't be seen, but I could hear the muffled sounds of baby raccoons whining in the background. Sally did come home to a place where she knew she was totally safe to give birth to her kittens. I was extremely happy not only for Sally, but for Punkin and myself as well. When Punkin arrived home on the bus after school, I met her in the front yard. Grasping her small hand in mine, we started toward Sally's barn. I had been afraid to just outright tell Punkin the news of Sally's joyful event. When we reached Sally's barn, I picked Punkin up and held her head close to the opening of the barn loft. I said, "Punkin, call for Sally, Honey, and then listen very carefully."

Punkin's soft voice called into the dark loft as if she were imitating my voice. Punkin gave a high pitched baby talk call saying, "Sally, are you home, Honey? Come out here."

Punkin's voice was rewarded with a chatter from Sally louder than the one I received when I called. Along with Sally's chatter were the whines of Sally's kittens. Punkin had been looking at my face as she made the call into Sally's loft. Suddenly, Punkin realized what she was hearing in the background of the dark loft. Punkin hadn't known what to expect when I led her out to Sally's barn, but she knew now. Punkin had heard those sounds before. The sounds Punkin heard from inside the loft were the exact sounds Sally made when she was a small, wrinkly, gray ball lying in the cotton lined shoe box. Punkin exploded, "Let's get Sally's babies out and look at them, Daddy," as she squirmed in my arms trying to get loose.

"Punkin, I don't think we should bother Sally or her babies right now. We need to let Sally rest for a few days because she has probably had a long trip trying to make it back home," I said.

A few minutes later, after Punkin and I had gone into the house, I could hear her rummaging through the junk drawer in the utility cabinet. Sitting in the recliner with my feet propped up reading the paper, I noticed Punkin out of the corner of my eye. She was standing with flashlight in hand and a look of, "Do I really have to ask?" on her face. I released the handle on the recliner, my feet flopped to the floor, I stood up and said, "Let's you and me go take a look, OK?"

I hated to admit it, but I was a little curious myself. I held Punkin high enough so she could shine the light in to the very of Sally's barn. There, in the middle of the hay pile Punkin and I had built, lay Sally. Sally had, without Punkin or myself knowing it, added a lot more hay and forest litter to her nest. Sally had accumulated a large pile of leaves and extra hay to make her nest larger. For the first time ever, I saw Sally's hair bristle on her back and neck. She gave a low growl as a notice that she would protect her kittens if necessary. Neither Punkin nor I could actually see Sally's kittens beneath the straw pile. We could detect a slight movement of the grass and hay in Sally's nest, but never actually got a glimpse of any of Sally's kittens.

After deciding we weren't going to get to see Sally's kittens without removing part of the loft door, Punkin and I returned to the big house. The next few hours were spent with Punkin using the phone advising all her friends and relatives of Sally's joyful event. If Punkin had been old enough to drive, I would have fully expected to see a sign in the rear window of her car the following day that read, "ASK ME ABOUT MY GRANDKIDS."

CHAPTER 20

Time seemed to pass slowly. Almost three weeks had passed since Sally had given birth to her kittens. Neither Punkin nor I had seen any of the kittens yet, even though we looked in Sally's loft on a regular basis, using the flashlight. Sally would occasionally come out to eat, but her mind was not really on playing with Punkin. Punkin and I were getting impatient. We both wanted to see the kittens. Late one evening after we had eaten supper, we decided to go out and check in on Sally and the kittens. I had taken the flashlight to look into the loft thinking I might catch the kittens uncovered or on top of the hay pile.

When we got to the barn, I picked Punkin up and shined the light to the back of the loft. There on top of the hay lay Sally. She was sprawled on her back with four tiny, dark raccoon kittens snuggled close to her underside. Each kitten was attached to a separate nipple on Sally's breast. I felt Punkin give a sigh and release a small breath.

"Oh, Daddy, they're so cute," she whispered. It was as if Punkin was congratulating Sally with her next statement. "Look, Daddy, they all look just like Sally!" she exclaimed.

From where I stood, all I could see were four tiny, dark, semi-hairy baby raccoon kittens, but I was not about to disagree with Punkin or the statement she just made. I had dealt with mothers and grandmothers before on the subject of kids and grandkids. So I said, "Yes, Honey, they all look just like Sally."

Over the next few weeks, the raccoon kittens began to play in the barn loft. Punkin would try each day to persuade one of the raccoon kittens to come close enough for her to touch it. The kittens were a lot more shy than Sally had been when she was that little. I attributed this to nature and some of the wild traits the kittens had gotten from their father. These very feelings of fear toward humans could possibly one day save their lives.

Although I stood and watched Punkin trying to calm those fears, I also knew that all humans did not have a heart like hers. There were still people around who could kill these raccoon kittens for sport.

The kittens finally grew big enough to come outside on their own and sun on the roof top of Sally's barn. Like Sally, when she was smaller, any loud noise or unfamiliar sight or sound would send them diving for the barn loft opening.

It was hilarious to watch four baby raccoons trying to get into the entrance to the loft all at the same time. Sometimes all we could see were four fat raccoon rumps, with furry tails attached, plugging the only entrance hole to the loft. One day while walking toward my warden truck, I noticed the entrance to Sally's barn loft was filled by four raccoon kitten heads. The little masked bandits were watching me intently as I made my way toward my truck. There was just enough room in the loft entrance that all four kittens could peek their heads out of the hole at the same time. I quickly turned toward the kittens and clapped my hands together loudly, and all four fuzzy heads disappeared at once.

91

Eventually, the kittens gained enough courage to venture down the locust pole to the ground below. As the kittens got older, Sally let Punkin pick up one or two of the kittens at a time to play with, but this made Sally extremely nervous. Anyone else touching one of the kittens was totally out of the question. I would squat and try to lure one of the kittens close to me, but Sally always placed herself between the closest kitten and me. She would give a low growling moan, bristle the hair on the back of her neck, and pace off a deliberate area between the kitten and me. It was like Sally was saying to me, "You can look, but you can't touch."

My satisfaction came in watching Punkin, Sally and the kittens rolling and frolicking at the base of the locust pole each evening. Never before had I known Punkin to be as content as she was when she was playing with Sally and the kittens.

CHAPTER 21

The rest of that summer seemed to be a sequel to the previous summer's events, except it was multiplied times four. Punkin would now take Sally and her family on hikes behind the big house along the dry creek bed. I watched as Punkin and Sally both tried to show the kittens how to survive in the wild. The previous summer's experiences worked fairly well on educating Punkin and Sally in how to get by in the wild.

Knowing all this life waving information was being passed on to Sally's kittens made me very happy. There were lessons in how to find food, how to climb trees, how to catch grasshoppers and crawfish, and how to relax and sleep in the sun after a hard day at work. The lesson they needed most, however, was not being taught – fear man and his beast.

Summer was coming to an end. The corn in the garden was more than six feet tall, and the stalks were beginning to turn brown. Sally's kittens were now half grown and, like Sally, the kittens had found that trickling water not only could be fun, but could be a valuable resource in the hot summertime. Punkin, Sally and the kittens spent the biggest majority of their time playing in and around the tall corn rows out in the garden.

When it was time for Punkin to return to school, Sally was not as upset as she had been the previous fall. She had plenty of things to keep her time occupied. Four—to be exact! Sally started taking her kittens on overnight stays out in the woods. On one of their return trips home, all four kittens and Sally had grape stains around their faces. Sally and the kittens had either been to my neighbor's grape vineyard or found some wild grapes along the creek bottom north of the big house. Either way I knew they were learning lessons in how to find food, even if it meant sneaking around someone else's house in the dark.

This habit of Sally leading her kittens away from home began to bother Punkin. Punkin even asked what she could do to make Sally and the kittens stay home. At this time, I reminded Punkin that Sally had made a choice between staying here or running free in the woods as a wild animal. Punkin finally understood it would be cruel to confine Sally to a cage, and I had made a vow to myself to never do that.

"Sally is far better off out roaming the woods with her kittens than sitting in a cage," I said.

For the first time, Punkin realized Sally was a wild animal and what it meant to be free. Punkin had given in to the idea that Sally and family were "Free Spirits." Punkin also knew Sally would occasionally return home for food and a safe place to sleep. She had always looked forward to Sally's precious visits, no matter how short they were. On some of Sally's later visits home, not all the kittens were with her. Some of Sally's kittens had evidently decided to try it in the wild on their own.

CHAPTER 22

At approximately 11:00 p.m. I stopped by the big house to grab a snack with me back to the deer woods. It was now early December. Although all the regular deer seasons were closed, I was still getting calls about deer poachers in different areas of my county. The phone rang as I started out the front door. Running back into the house, I picked up the phone as quickly as possible so the ringing wouldn't wake Punkin or her mother.

The voice on the other end of the line said, "Dekota, this is Alva Powers. I have some people running dogs in the canyon down here below my house, so if you possibly could come over here and check them out, I would appreciate it. This home place is posted, plus I have cattle on this place, and no one is supposed to be hunting down there."

"OK! I'll be right there," I replied.

The man on the phone was my closest neighbor. He lived less than two miles straight west of where we lived in the big house. I arrived at the gate to Alva's property in less than ten minutes after receiving his call. From where I was standing at the entrance gate to Mr. Power's property, I could hear the bellowing of the hounds farther west. I started down the main creek toward where the hounds were barking. By the hounds' excitement, I knew they had already treed whatever they were chasing. It took about ten more minutes to close the distance between the dogs and me. From where I now stood, I could see beams of light being flashed up into the tree tops in the same area where the hounds were bellowing. I could see about three-fourths of the way up into the tree above the hounds. There, among the limbs and branches, appeared to be the outline of a human. One of the hunters was standing directly beneath the tree talking to the hunter up in the tree.

"Kick that one there and make it jump out," he yelled.

One of the other hunters below was blowing a raccoon squaller. This raccoon squaller made the sound of a raccoon being killed. The squaller would give high pitched squeals and squalls that would make the raccoon in the tree think the dogs on the ground were already in the act of killing another raccoon. This false sense of security would make the treed raccoon jump out of the tree to try to escape while the dogs below killed the other raccoon, when in all reality, there was no other raccoon. Therefore, when the treed raccoon jumped out of the tree, it was actually jumping to its death.

I closed in to within about forty yards of the hunters and their dogs. Before approaching these subjects in the dark, I stopped to catch my breath. While I stopped and caught my breath, the person in the tree managed to kick the raccoon out of the upper branches where it had been hiding. The raccoon landed with a loud "thud" among the hounds waiting below. Taking off at a full run, I wanted to get to the hounds before they killed the raccoon. I never made it. On my way to the dogs, I ran past one hunter, but I was already too late to save the small raccoon. All five dogs attacked the small raccoon the second it impacted the ground. The hounds had within a few seconds torn the half-grown raccoon to pieces. I could literally hear bones being crushed in the small raccoon's body as each hound took its turn at mauling the helpless body.

I told the subjects to catch their dogs and chain them. I asked the hunters for their hunting licenses, and all three subjects produced one. I then asked, "Do you have permission to hunt on this particular piece of property?"

"Hell, it's coon season, ain't it!" the biggest hunter replied.

"Yes, it is," I replied, "but do you have permission to hunt here?"

The next reply was one that I heard from coon hunters too many times over the last sixteen years.

"We been huntin' here for twenty years. We come from down the creek. We didn't see no signs. Besides my dogs can't read them signs anyway," the big man said. Then all three men gave a guttural laugh.

I told all three hunters they were hunting without permission even though it was raccoon season. Taking some information from the hunter's licenses, I made out each hunter a citation for hunting without the landowner's permission. As I finished the citations, the question arose as to the cost of the fine. I advised the three subjects, "The cost will be around $87 each. You will need to the contact the people in the court house at our county seat to pay the fines."

The hunters retrieved their dogs and started to leave. I asked, "Aren't you going to take the raccoon with you that your dogs killed so you can skin and sell the hide?"

Their response was, "Hides aren't worth messing with." That meant they were killing the raccoons simply for the sport of the hunt.

As if to slur me personally, one of the hunters said, "Two up and two down."

Then as all three hunters started to leave, the older hunter in the bunch shined his head lamp on the carcass of the half-grown raccoon and gave it a kick.

"Coon huntin's a hell of a sport, ain't it, Warden?" he asked and then laughed aloud again. As all three hunters passed the lifeless body, each hunter's dog gave the raccoon carcass a shake. At the older hunter's statement, I thought to myself that ignorance and inhumanity aren't virtues for someone to brag about.

When the hunters were out of sight, I began my routine of burying the half-grown raccoon the dogs killed and the hunters left to waste. Completely covering the grave site with leaves and sticks, I started back down the canyon toward the creek. I was going to follow the creek back to the main road where I left my truck. Then I realized what the hunters were actually insinuating with their remarks. "Two up and two down" meant they had probably killed another raccoon before I actually made it to the scene. Immediately I started searching the area to see if my instincts were correct. Sure enough after searching just a couple of minutes, I spied a large bundle of brown fur closer to the creeks edge. Approaching the site of the kill, I put my light on the large raccoon. I thought to myself this must have been the mother because the body of this raccoon was three times as large as the young raccoon I just buried. Placing my right boot under the large, bloody bundle, I turned it over. Instantly my heart tightened into a large knot and sank to my stomach. There in the dim light was a perfect, white triangle in the center of the raccoon's throat. The large raccoon that lay at my feet was Sally.

As I went to my knees, my eyes swelled with tears. Carefully I placed my hands under Sally and scooped up her limp body from the ground. I could barely catch my breath as I cradled her like a baby in my arms. A thousand thoughts raced through my mind. Most of the thoughts were about all the love and joy Sally had brought to our lives during the time Punkin and I raised her. I wanted to feel Sally's cool paws reach out and rub my face, but I knew that was impossible. My heart became a puzzle that had been broken into a thousand tiny pieces. I knew no matter how or when I put it back together, there would still be a small missing piece right in the center.

As I sat in the dark holding Sally, I thought of the hunters and how just one selfish act destroyed not only a beautiful raccoon but years of childhood memories for one small nine year old girl. As I was thinking, I spoke out loud, "If I hurt this bad, what will this senseless act do to Punkin?"

With Sally still cradled in my arms, I headed down the creek to my truck. It was one of the longest walks of my life. When I finally arrived back at the truck, I placed Sally in the floor board on the passenger's side of my truck and started home. I still hadn't decided what to do about Sally. All the thoughts racing through my head weren't perfectly clear. As I pulled to one side of the road, I clinched my fist tightly around each side of the steering wheel and laid my forehead against the top of the wheel. Exactly how long I sat there, I don't know. I thought of how things used to be and how I wanted things to be now. After a while, reality set in, and I had to look at the way things really were. As I wiped the tears from my cheeks, I thought to myself that I really needed to make a plan and follow through with it.

The plan that came to mind was that Sally should go back where I found her over two years ago. I would take Sally back and bury her as close to her mother's grave as possible in Mr. Crowe's creek bottom.

CHAPTER 23

Closing the wire gate behind my truck, I slowly traveled the old sandy road beside the creek meandering through Mr. Crowe's property. The road was still damp from the midnight dew. My truck was making very little noise except for the tall weeds that grew between the ruts and were now striking the bottom of my truck as I drove over them. The spot where I found Sally tow and one-half years earlier was fast approaching. I managed to drive within thirty yards of where the poachers cut down the raccoon den tree from which I had earlier retrieved Sally. I took my flashlight out of the truck and started to look for a grave site for Sally. In some taller grass, I came across the tree den tree where I found Sally when she was a baby. After looking around at the base of the den tree, I could see a wood rat had built a nest of limbs, sticks and seed pods that he had stored for the coming winter. The rat's nest was mounded up high all around the hollow end of the log that was once Sally's home. Even after all the damage done by the poachers, there was still some good to come out of them trying to destroy the raccoons' den tree. The fallen tree had become home to a large family of wood rats. Slowly I walked in the direction of where I thought I placed Sally's mother's grave. There in the edge of the grass pasture stood a lone elm branch at the head of a small mound of dirt covered with last fall's dried, brown leaves. The horizontal branch of the cross was no longer attached to the lone stick. Returning quickly to my truck, I retrieved a shovel along with Sally. Sally

101

was still warm and limp. I hurried to get my job done as fast as I possibly could, so I wouldn't actually think about what I was doing. After I rounded and patted the dirt on Sally's grave, I stood in silence for a moment in thought. I had made the grave and placed Sally as close to her mother as possible without disturbing the mother's grave.

Then I said aloud, "I've brought your baby back to you. I tried my very best to keep her safe, but Sally wanted to be free. She turned out to be quite a little lady. Everyone that knew her loved her and she touched all our lives with love." Then I took a deep breath, turned and walked away. On my way back to my warden truck, I really had only one thought, "How can I ever tell Punkin about Sally?"

THE NEXT SUMMER

Steam sizzled from the muffler of my game warden truck as I hit the small puddles of water left on the black asphalt road from the welcomed early summer shower. My attention seemed to drawn toward the horizon on my left. The sun was setting and it would be totally dark in less than thirty minutes. From the reddish tint already appearing on the higher clouds, I knew tomorrow would be a beautiful day. Over the years, my 101 year old grandmother convinced me that "a red sky at night was indeed a sailor's delight."

The big house was coming into view. Punkin was sitting on the front steps of the wooden porch. As I neared the driveway to the big house, Punkin jumped to her feet and started running at full speed toward the end of the driveway. Punkin's long thin arms were flailing about as she made large outward circles with them, while at the same time jumping as high as she could into the air. My heart raced at the sight because I thought something bad might have happened to Punkin or her mother. Yet the closer I got, it was very plain to see that Punkin was just filled with excitement. Punkin managed to make her run to about halfway down the drive to meet me before I had to bring the truck to a complete stop. Punkin and I both stopped moving; we were now face to face. Punkin stood directly in front of my truck. Her full length blonde hair was being swept across her face by the wind. This made her high cheek bones and perfectly pointed chin become even more prominent. Although I was her dad, I hadn't really noticed up until now that during the last three years she had lost her little round baby face. She was turning into a young lady, and honestly she was beautiful! I turned the ignition off on my truck and started to step out. Punkin met me at the door of the truck with a high pitched enthusiastic voice. Reaching down and grabbing my hand, Punkin pulled me toward the front of my truck.

"Quick, Daddy, come look out in the garden," she squealed.

Punkin was pulling on my hand practically dragging me toward the garden. Just to keep up, I had to quicken my normal pace. When we reached the garden, Punkin exclaimed, "Look, Daddy, look!" as she pointed to the ground.

In the middle of the corn rows were dozens of tiny hand prints. These tiny raccoon tracks had been left by the previous night's visitors. With Punkin's small, thin finger pointing down at the tracks, she asked, "Daddy, do you think these are Sally's tracks?"

I hesitated a moment and said, "I don't think so, Honey. Sally's tracks would probably be much larger than those. These tracks probably belong to three or four younger raccoons. Punkin stared quietly at the ground. I could feel her disappointment in my answer as her enthusiasm faded. Then Punkin asked the question I had feared she would someday ask. I had been rehearsing an answer to this question over and over in my mind for almost a year.

"Daddy, whatever happened to Sally?" Punkin asked.

So Punkin couldn't see my face, I turned my head away. No matter what answers I had practiced in the past year, they all seemed to vanish the very instant

Punkin's question came out of her mouth. I never wanted to be the person to give Punkin her first broken heart. All the memories of Sally and Punkin flashed through my mind as I reached down and turned Punkin's body to face mine.

"I have to tell you something, Punkin," I said.

I tried hard to swallow the knot that had come up into my throat. No matter how hard I tried to swallow, the knot kept coming back up. Bending over, I caught Punkin under the arm pits as if I were pulling Sally from the small barn loft and lifted Punkin to my chest. Punkin immediately locked her arms around my neck and at the same moment locked her long, thin legs around my waist. Punkin buried her head against my neck and I gave her a long hard squeeze. Pressed against me like this, I could feel Punkin's tiny heart thumping against my chest. After a long silent hesitation, Punkin leaned her head back and stared directly into my eyes. Her lips were clinched tightly together, and her eyes were already filling with tears in preparation for the answer she feared was forthcoming. Staring deep into my watering eyes, she waited for her answer. After swallowing hard, I took in a deep breath of air to hold the knot down. At the same time, I was uncontrollably shuffling my body. Then as I pointed, I said, "Punkin turn around and look over here."

In the west the sun had already gone down below the horizon. The disappearing sun left long, straight, beautiful streaks of pink, blue and gray in the evening sky.

I softly said, "Punkin, do you remember when you go to Sunday School and you hear the teachers talk about how safe and peaceful Heaven is?"

I could see Punkin's mind wandering off as she said, "Yes."

"Well, Punkin," I said, "I want you to know that wherever Sally is now there are beautiful clear creeks with plenty of flat rocks and lots of crawfish under every rock. Sally can spend all her time doing what she always liked best, and that was fishing. So from now on, when you think of Sally, I want you to remember Sally's in a very special place where no man or dog can ever hurt her."

There was a silent pause while she thought about what I said. Punkin had drawn her own final conclusions on "What ever Happened to Sally."

Punkin leaned over close to me and gave me a tight hug around the neck.

"I love you, Daddy," Punkin said softly. I swallowed hard again trying to keep that knot from coming back up into my throat.

Then I squeezed Punkin close again, softly kissed her cheek and whispered, "I love you, too, Punkin."

I set her down, and she trotted off toward the big house with her golden hair blowing in the wind.

ABOUT THE AUTHOR

My name is Dekota R. Cagle and I am a Captain with the Oklahoma Department of Wildlife with twenty-four-years of service. I am stationed in western Oklahoma along the South Canadian River in Caddo County. My book is a true story of my then six-year-old daughter and I raising a raccoon over a three-year period.

www.ingramcontent.com/pod-product-compliance
Lightning Source LLC
Chambersburg PA
CBHW031229280526
45784CB00004B/1503